"*We'll All Be Free* serves as a kind yet stirring reminder that there are no winners under white supremacy's weight. Throughout these pages, you'll find Caroline to be a comforter, cheerleader, and coach for the journey ahead. Get ready to look backward to see the truth of our history, inward to unlearn the lies we believe, and forward to work toward a bright, free future."

Danielle Coke, illustrator and activist

"At several points throughout *We'll All Be Free*, I would pause and hover over a sentence, trying to memorize what Caroline had to say because I didn't want to simply highlight her words; I wanted to let her ideas and insights sink deep within, to continue to stir and challenge me long after I put the book down. Weaving her own story of adoption and trauma and pain, Caroline makes connections to concepts such as white supremacy culture in a fresh and compelling way. This book will help you understand not just what is broken in our racist and patriarchal society but how it connects to your own story. As a white woman and a recovering perfectionist, I am so grateful this book exists."

Jenny Booth Potter, author of *Doing Nothing Is No Longer an Option*

"In *We'll All Be Free*, Caroline J. Sumlin writes, 'For us to heal, to reclaim our worth, we must not only dig deep enough to discover the roots of our collective feelings of unworthiness but also dig deep enough to pull them all out together. . . . Remember, we cannot actively uproot a problem if we cannot find the roots to begin with.' Equal parts historical retelling, memoir, and roadmap, *We'll All Be Free* is one of a kind. Sumlin prompts readers to grasp at the roots of our own personal traumas and then draws explicit connections between feelings of unworthiness and the insidiousness of white supremacy culture, which has shaped each of us from our earliest

memories. Sumlin asks all of us to uproot internalized feelings of inferiority and self-doubt within the context of the perfectionism and toxic bootstrapping of white supremacy culture. *We'll All Be Free* is both expansive and intimate; it is sweeping in its historical research and also breathtaking in its rawness and vulnerability. Sumlin's debut work is a must-read for . . . well, all of us."

Kate Slater, PhD, racial justice scholar and educator

We'll
All Be
Free

We'll All Be *Free*

How a Culture of White Supremacy Devalues Us and How We Can Reclaim Our True Worth

Caroline J. Sumlin

BakerBooks

a division of Baker Publishing Group
Grand Rapids, Michigan

Published by Baker Books
a division of Baker Publishing Group
Grand Rapids, Michigan
www.bakerbooks.com

Printed in the United States of America

Library of Congress Cataloging-in-Publication Data
Names: Sumlin, Caroline J., 1990– author.
Title: We'll all be free : how a culture of white supremacy devalues us and how we can reclaim our true worth / Caroline J. Sumlin.
Other titles: We will all be free
Description: Grand Rapids, Michigan : Baker Books, a division of Baker Publishing Group, [2023] | Includes bibliographical references.
Identifiers: LCCN 2022048113 | ISBN 9781540902894 (paperback) | ISBN 9781540903211 (casebound) | ISBN 9781493441174 (ebook)
Subjects: LCSH: United States—Race relations. | Racism—United States. | African Americans—Civil rights. | African Americans—Social conditions. | Self-esteem. | Sumlin, Caroline J., 1990—Psychology.
Classification: LCC E185.615 .S86 2023 | DDC 305.800973—dc23/eng/20221011
LC record available at https://lccn.loc.gov/2022048113

Published in association with The Bindery Agency, www.TheBinderyAgency.com.

Baker Publishing Group publications use paper produced from sustainable forestry practices and post-consumer waste whenever possible.

23   24   25   26   27   28   29   7   6   5   4   3   2   1

*To every single person who's ever whispered
to themselves, "I'll never be enough."*
You have always been enough. I hope this book
helps you come home to who you've always been.

To my husband.
You believed in me in my darkest hours, you pushed me when I
wanted to quit, you sacrificed your time so I could have just a few
more hours to write, and you loved me harder when I was most
unlovable. Without you, these pages would not exist. I love you.

To my girls.
You learned to play quietly so Mama could finish up just a
few more paragraphs, you gave more grace than I deserved
when stress got the best of me, and you cheered me on
and told everyone I was the "best writer in the whole wide
world." Most importantly, you always fill my days with
more laughter and love than I could ever imagine. I hope
your memories of these moments light a fire in your bellies
to pursue your wildest dreams. Mama loves you.

To my mom.
You taught me to be strong, be independent, and never
settle. You taught me to dare to thrive in a world that was
built to make our mere survival nearly impossible. Thank
you for always pushing me to a potential I couldn't see.

To my dad.
Watching you choose work that lit your soul on fire gave
me permission to do the same. I miss you every day.

Contents

Prelude 11

Part 1 The Foundation

1. Our Primal Wound 25
2. They Didn't Know Better 40
3. Never Enough 53

Part 2 Reclaiming Our Worth

4. Where We First Learned to Be White 83
5. U.G.L.Y. 108
6. Hustle 131
7. The Crisis We Refuse to See 156

Part 3 Finding Freedom

8. Stop Chasing 175
9. Breaking the Cycle 189
10. We'll All Be Free 202

Epilogue 221
For Further Reading 225
Acknowledgments 227
Notes 229

Prelude

We live in a world that does not value us for who we are. When did you first realize this truth? I'll never forget the day it became a reality for me. It was the day I realized I was Black.

I was in kindergarten. My best friend (who was also Black) and I were playing during recess. Our braids bounced freely as we chased each other around and around before ending up on the ground, our little bodies overcome by laughter. We were in a world of our own, without care. I then led the way toward my favorite slide. It was one of those tunnel slides that are so dark as you go down that you get lost for a moment until you come out the other side.

I eagerly ran up to the entrance of the slide, but a voice stopped me.

"Get out of my way, you BLACK GIRL!"

I lost my breath for a moment as I saw a white boy staring at me with hatred on his face. I couldn't move. I knew he wasn't calling me a Black girl just to point out that I happened to be Black. He was calling me a Black girl to emphasize that I had no business being in *his* way, sharing *his* playground, going down a slide that *he* wanted.

He was calling me a Black girl because he believed that, as a white boy, he was better than me.

He pushed me out of the way and slid down. My friend immediately ran to tell the teacher. I couldn't move, though. Overcome with shock, I sat on the ground, trying to catch my breath and wrap my mind around what had just happened. A lump rose in my throat, but I didn't cry. I just . . . sat.

That was when I learned that being Black didn't just mean that my skin happened to be brown but also that I would forever be perceived as "less than" everyone else in the world.

If I'm being totally honest, I had already sensed that my Blackness wasn't just different from most of what I saw around me; it also wasn't "as good as being white." I had already sensed this because it was everywhere. It was inescapable.

I was one of only two Black girls in my entire kindergarten class, and the two of us were best friends. We immediately gravitated toward each other when we met in orientation because we saw ourselves when we looked at each other. We saw chocolate skin while everyone else had vanilla. We saw thick, textured, plaited hair while everyone else had slick, straight hair that moved with the wind. We heard the sameness in our voices while everyone else's intonation was just a bit . . . different. We didn't know the decisions our subconscious brains were making, but we knew we felt safe with each other. Somehow, we knew the world that surrounded us *wasn't made for us.*

I always subconsciously knew what it meant to be Black, even at the tender age of five. Unless I was with my Black mother, attending our historic Black church in St. Paul, Minnesota, whiteness was everywhere. It was in every store, on the cover of every magazine, and on every television show. It was in the faces of my teachers, classmates, and the pictures in all my textbooks. I knew Blackness was different. I knew it wasn't seen as being as pretty or as smart as whiteness. My little brain couldn't articulate that, but I *knew*.

However, that day on the playground made what I had sensed *real*. It confirmed my feelings and turned them into truth.

Once your eyes are opened to a truth, it becomes impossible to close them. Once you know, you see it everywhere. From that moment, there was no escaping the fact that I was Black and there was no escaping the message that surrounded me that "**Whiteness is better.**"

———

Before I go any further, let me introduce myself. Hi, my name is Caroline. I'm a thirtysomething wife and homeschooling mama of two who has fumbled around most of my life feeling like a worthless mistake. Maybe you can relate to that. Until recently, the only language I was fluent in was self-hate. You'll learn more about my story as you read this book. Right now, I want to thank you for being here. Thank you for trusting my flawed, passionate self to help you on your own self-worth journey. Thank you for choosing to let me in. Thank you for trusting me.

You may be feeling a tad confused right now, asking yourself, *Did I pick up a book about racism, white supremacy, or self-worth?*

Yes. All of the above.

You may also be asking yourself, *Is this book for me? Or is this book for Black women? Or white women? Black men, maybe?*

Yes. This book is for everyone.

Am I safe here?

That is my number one goal.

You are here because you are ready to reclaim your self-worth. Once and for all. If you're like me, you've tried everything else. You've tried manifesting it, hoping that if you just think your way into loving yourself, you'll finally love yourself. You've tried praying for your self-worth, only to feel immense disappointment the moment you finish your prayer and unworthiness hits you like a ton of bricks . . . again. You've tried faking it until you make it. You've tried avoidance. And most of all, you've probably spent your whole life *chasing after it.*

Chasing it with perfectionism.

Chasing it by hustling.

Chasing it with titles and status.

Chasing it with low-calorie diets and skinny teas.

Chasing it with Instagram filters and the perfect contour.

Chasing it with flawless church attendance.

Chasing it by chasing after every single standard society tells you will finally make you feel *good enough.*

And now you are here. Because you are tired of chasing. You're out of breath. You're over it. And every manifestation and affirmation has done diddly-squat. So you picked up this book, hoping and *begging* that it will finally lead you *somewhere.*

This time you aren't manifesting and you aren't chasing. You are uncovering the *truth* about the root of your battle with unworthiness, and that root is white supremacy culture.

In this book, we will dissect the different ways white supremacy culture has led to **every single one of us believing an inherent lie of self-unworthiness** as it has attempted to destroy the minds and bodies of those who are Black, Indigenous, People of Color (BIPOC), as well as every other marginalized community. Together we will deconstruct the lies white supremacy culture has fed us so we can break free from the chains of unworthiness that are weighing us down and walk in the true liberation we all deserve.

I promise that if you stick with me, you will not only see white supremacy in a completely new light but also see yourself in a completely new light. You will be able to see the person who has been hidden inside you since the moment the world began tainting your perception and you began to believe the lie that you aren't good enough.

⸻

Growing up, I used to think that my struggles with unworthiness were unique to me, my childhood trauma, and the unfortunate cards I'd been dealt. I thought I was the only one who felt this deep self-loathing. Everyone else seemed to totally love and believe in themselves and have their self-worth game down. It wasn't until recently that I realized we are all walking through different versions of the unworthiness battle.

We are all chasing worth and validation because our society was intentionally built to keep us chasing.

Our collective struggle with self-worth is so ingrained in us that it shows up in ways we have completely normalized as a society. Imposter syndrome, self-doubt, a constant striving for achievement and perfection, feeling guilty for resting or not being productive, feeling guilty for asking for help, putting ourselves last, living in fear, and having to announce and qualify a need for self-care so we can justify that we, in fact, earned that self-care—these are all ways unworthiness infiltrates our daily lives. We are all living through the lens of having something to prove, as if just living is not good enough.

You may be nodding your head in agreement right now as you recognize yourself in this collective battle with unworthiness, but you may also be wondering what in the world this has to do with white supremacy.

Traditionally we have been taught that white supremacy only exists within the realm of the KKK and other white nationalist groups that represent extreme ideals within our society. The idea that white supremacy is something found in more than just a few extremist groups is one that most of us are just beginning to grapple with, let alone understand how much it has deeply affected all of us to our detriment.

Before we go any further, we need to accurately define *white supremacy* and *white supremacy culture.*

White supremacy is

[A] political, economic and cultural system in which whites over-whelmingly control power and material resources, conscious and unconscious ideas of white superiority and entitlement are wide-spread, and relations of white dominance and non-white subordination are daily reenacted across a broad array of institutions and social settings.[1]

This is the system our Western society has been built upon since the earliest days of colonization, when the concepts of race and whiteness were created to justify colonization and the institution of chattel slavery. This system is so normalized and ingrained within us that we must willfully take off our collective blindfold to see it. Once that blindfold is removed, we will see that it's not only everywhere but is the literal *definition* of the society we live in.

White supremacy is like the brick foundation that our home (our nation and the Western world) was built on top of. The pillars of our society are also white supremacy, as systems and structures have continued to be created throughout our four-hundred-year history to ensure it is always upheld. This foundation and these pillars have created our entire culture: the house of white supremacy in which we all live. There is a world that exists outside this house, but unless we open the door and fully step outside, we will never see it.

White supremacy, in conjunction with our capitalist society, is the overarching system that reproduces and reinforces other systems of oppression such as classism, sexism, heterosexism, ageism, and ableism. Each of these systems strategically marginalizes and dehumanizes one group of people to protect and maintain the power of another group of people. From these systems of oppression, which flow through our society the same way blood flows through our veins, emerges *white supremacy culture.* The *system* of white supremacy is what creates **white supremacy culture.**

Let's take a quick look at the Merriam-Webster definition of *culture*:

> Culture: the customary beliefs, social norms, and material traits of a racial, religious or social group.
>
> *Also:* the characteristic features of everyday existence (such as diversions or way of life) shared by people in a place or time.[2]

While Western society is a conglomeration of many different cultures, we cannot forget we also exist under one umbrella, which is an overarching white supremacy, or white dominant, culture we all have had no choice but to succumb to. The systems of white supremacy have created norms, customs, values, beliefs, and standards that have taught us that whiteness is better, whiteness is success, and whiteness is value—and unless you assimilate yourself to strive for whiteness, you are forever not good enough.[3] This is white supremacy culture.

We have one more definition to comprehend before we continue, and that is the definition of *whiteness.* I completely understand this may make you want to run if you are a white person who is reading this. I know this can be a sensitive topic. But do me a favor and bear with me.

White supremacy was developed out of the concept and belief that whiteness is superior to all other races and/or ethnicities. In short, *whiteness* is the absence of Blackness. Since the creation of race, Blackness has been considered the lowest tier of humanity in our society and whiteness has always been the top tier, with every other race falling somewhere along this spectrum. This is why the definitions of success, beauty, status, and value have always been assigned to the white population.

Besides the obvious discriminatory problem with this, the standard of whiteness has become a standard that is nearly impossible for anyone to achieve—white people included. This one standard—of success, of beauty, of intelligence, of value—leaves 99 percent of the population believing there is something wrong with them if they don't achieve it. In order to justify the chase to achieve that one standard, a culture of white supremacy emerged, and within it, toxic characteristics of white supremacy culture have become our norm.

As we go on, you will learn what those toxic characteristics are and how they have contributed to the beliefs we have about ourselves that lead us to say, "I'm not enough."

It may be difficult to comprehend how a societal structure that was originally built to marginalize and suppress its Black and Indigenous populations could also harm everyone else under its domain. Maybe you were even tempted to put this book down as you read the previous sentences, assuming that this book is not written for you. I'm glad you didn't heed that temptation, because this book is for all of us.

White supremacy culture has taken our humanity away from us. Every single system that falls under the umbrella of white supremacy has confused us into believing that our humanity and our worth are conditional, and we've honestly fallen for it. We have cultivated a culture that has abused power, neglected emotions and trauma, degraded people for having imperfections, and dehumanized us for our differences. Every single one of us is affected by this. Whether you're Black, white, male, female, or something in between, you have more than likely believed you have to *do more* and *be more* to be worthy of love, freedom, abundance, or joy.

If we don't fight these systems and beliefs that have told us for too long that our worth is conditional on our achievement and our whiteness, we will collapse. Heartache, trauma, and oppression will break us down, and there will be no standing up again.

On January 6, 2021, I woke up.

I woke up to the reality of America. When I saw that evil, terrifying display of white supremacy as an angry mob stormed our nation's Capitol, everything changed for me. That was the moment I realized I had been trying my entire life to exist in a world that was strategically built against me. Those kindergarten realizations were confirmed once again. This world didn't want me. And I would never be good enough for it because I would always be Black, and I would always be a woman, and I would always be a Black woman. No amount of "progress" this country seemingly made was ever going to change the fact that white supremacy would always win.

You would think that these feelings would have driven me to throw in the towel. What was the point of fighting anymore? White supremacy had won. And I was tired.

I was tired of being Black. I was tired of being Black in America. I was tired of swallowing my pain. I was tired of holding back tears. I was tired of always having to prove myself. I was tired of constantly feeling unworthy of my humanity.

I had a choice to make. I could let the weight crush me. Or I could unapologetically start screaming and let the weight gradually fall off my shoulders with every scream.

I chose the latter. I started speaking up. I started talking about racism and white supremacy and how they have tried to destroy us for far too long. I began recognizing just how big of an impact white supremacy and racism have had on my life. An impact I once dismissed as normal and had faulted myself for not being strong enough to deal with.

The more I cried and spoke out, the more revelation I received. I began digging into the research, desperate for answers for the pain white supremacy has caused me and my BIPOC brothers and sisters. I began learning about exactly what white supremacy is, the culture it created in our society, and how it has crippled not only BIPOC lives but the lives of every single one of us.

I don't know your story. I don't know how you're feeling, what you've gone through, or how our society has played a role in your personal experiences. What I can say is that as a society we have shut down humanity for far too long, and it cannot go on any longer. We each deserve to walk in the fullness of our humanity, our broken pieces and battle scars on full display without shame, healing without apology, and paving the way for the cycles of dehumanization to finally end.

Let's make our generation the last generation that ever has to feel ashamed of their humanity. Let's make our generation the last generation that ever has to question the worthiness of our existence.

Enough is enough.

It's our turn to take on this world and create lasting change that says, "Oppression has no place here. Marginalization has no place here. Dehumanization has no place here."

Only humanity has a place here. Only equity has a place here. Only love has a place here. Only freedom has a place here.

There was a "you" that existed before you began hiding. By the end of this book, you will have begun to be reacquainted with this person you never even knew you were searching for.

Here's what you can expect as we embark on this journey. I've broken this book up into three parts. In part 1, you will learn about how white supremacy was constructed and how that led to the culture of white supremacy we live in today. You will also begin to make connections to how the foundation of white supremacy is directly correlated to the roots of your own feelings of unworthiness. You will also learn a lot of accurate, truthful history throughout this book—but no worries, I've written it in such a way that it is interesting and digestible. I bet you'll want to dig further into many of the topics we discuss, which I highly encourage. In my opinion, history is always the missing piece of the puzzle that is staring us right in the face as we look high and low trying to search for it. Also, at the end of each chapter are a few journal prompts to help you digest what you've learned and take actionable steps toward reclaiming your true worth.

Part 2 looks at a few major sectors of society that are constantly telling us we are never enough: the school system, the beauty and diet industry, and hustle culture. You will learn the specific white supremacist roots of each of these sectors and how those roots have led these sectors to be the primary drivers of the white supremacy culture machine, thus further increasing the unworthiness you feel. Most importantly, you will begin to see the full picture coming together, from the lies you have been told that have disguised themselves as standards to the truths you can begin replacing those lies with. You will start to feel a weight lift from your shoulders.

In part 3, you will find freedom. You will take actionable steps that will help you break up with white supremacy culture for good, reclaim the worth it has stolen from you, walk in true freedom, and work toward doing the redemptive work of creating a future that is free from the chains of white supremacy. This book will give you the tools you need to get started as well as pointing you toward more tools to add to your liberation tool kit. You will have what you need to fight the battle for your mental health and your liberation and to finally be able to look in the mirror and say "I love me" without reserve.

Always remember, you are safe here. This is a journey. It is not a race. Take your time but stay consistent. Even if you have to pick this book back up twenty-five times, just make sure you keep picking it back up. I will be here with you every step of the way. We are on this journey together. While I may be a few steps ahead of you, reaching back and taking your hand, I am still walking along the same path. It is a path that does not end on this side of heaven. It is a lifelong journey, a lifelong commitment to healing, fighting, resting, and declaring our liberation.

You've got this. I promise.

Part 1

The Foundation

1

Our Primal Wound

I don't know much about the day I was born.

I know the date and the time. I know some of the names of the people involved. But other than that, I don't have a lot of information.

That always bothered me.

Most people know how much they weighed at birth. I don't. Most people know how much hair they had on their heads. I don't. Most people know the details of their birth story, because their mothers were able to relive that day and share it with them. Not me. I've never had a story. Just a few pieces of paper: an original birth certificate and a few handwritten forms that reveal so little information you would think they were trying to keep a secret.

One day, shortly after I turned sixteen, my adoptive mother told me she had something to give me. She went to the depths of the basement while I sat feeling confused, twiddling my thumbs and anxiously waiting to see what she had for me. There was something about my birthday that always reignited my adoption curiosity, which led me to inundate my mother with questions around the same time every year. Was I finally going to get some new answers?

She returned with a thin manila folder in her hand. "These are your adoption papers," she said. "Now that you're sixteen, I think you're old enough to have them."

Looking down at my toes, I inhaled, taking a deep, shaky breath that I tried to hide. Emotion filled the pit of my stomach, but I couldn't let it bubble over. Showing my emotions in front of others, especially my mom, was a huge no-no for me.

"Thank you," I responded, slowly reaching to take the folder from her hands.

Inhaling again, this time a little less shakily, I opened it. This wasn't the first time I was hearing about my adoption, but it was the first time I had seen any official documentation about it.

Until then, I had always summarized my adoption story in a few sentences: "I was born in New York. My parents were mentally challenged, so they couldn't take care of me. My grandmother took care of me until my mom adopted me when I was two and a half."

Imagine a five-year-old girl reciting these lines when asked. I didn't understand what it all meant, but I recited this narrative with confidence as if I were perfectly content with the adoption and had no questions whatsoever about the details of my story.

Except I *did* have questions. Questions that plagued me, such as, *Did my mother scream when they took me away? Why couldn't she take care of me? What does "mentally challenged" mean? Why am I here? Am I a mistake?*

Those questions lingered in my mind as I walked the giggle-filled hallways at school, stroked a yellow tennis ball during tennis practice, and cried myself to sleep at night when my existence felt like the biggest disappointment.

As a young child, I didn't have the words to articulate this, but at my core, I had felt like a mistake for as long as I could remember. Everyone I knew had two parents who lived together. But I had always lived with only one parent. My adoptive father lived across town, and while I saw him often and he was a pillar of strength in my life, I was still envious of those who had the privilege of both parents tucking them in every night. Plus, their parents had been theirs from the beginning. They had been born to and allowed to go home with the *same* parents. They didn't have to "earn their parents" like I did. They didn't have to "wait for love" as I had. They didn't have a big black hole at the beginning of their story.

But I did. I had a void that made me question the worthiness of my existence from my earliest memories. This void whispered to me daily.

You aren't supposed to be here.

You are a mistake.

Your mother is going to send you back.

She doesn't really love you.

These whispers threatened my childhood innocence, sense of wonder, and ultimately my self-worth.

What I didn't realize at that time was that those words were a response to trauma. I didn't know that very real psychological trauma occurs when babies are separated from their biological mothers. Their responses mimic what occurs when someone experiences the death of a parent.[1] And if a baby continues to experience trauma during infancy and toddlerhood, that trauma is more psychologically detrimental than trauma experienced during later stages of childhood due to the vital brain development occurring in those first years.[2]

I didn't know I had experienced a primal wound. I didn't know that my birth itself was traumatic and that I would be left picking up the pieces for the rest of my life. I didn't know that my infant and toddler years had also been harrowing. To my adoptive mother's best recollection, I had spent them in a pseudo–foster care situation, abandoned in a crib for hours at a time. (The story that my biological grandmother had taken care of me for two years turned out to be mostly untrue.) I didn't realize that my heart had already shattered into a million pieces before I had seen my third birthday.

The moment I laid eyes on those papers, the reality of the trauma I had endured hit me like a jolt of lightning. Emotion continued to rush through my body like a tidal wave, but I kept my facial expression stoic as I read and reread my original birth certificate with a stranger's name listed where it said "mother." My stomach felt as though I was riding a roller coaster, and I hated roller coasters. I could not stop staring at this woman's name. I had heard that name before. Anytime I asked my adoptive mother questions about my adoption, she never hesitated to offer what details she knew. She'd told me the name of both my biological mother and father before, but something about seeing their names on this document from the day of my birth made what happened to me so real. There was really a woman out there who had carried me for nine months, only for us to not continue our lives together as most babies and mothers get to do.

I was beginning to realize that I had experienced trauma. Trauma I had spent an entire childhood waving off as "normal," as if it had no effect on me. Until then, I thought my feelings of unworthiness were my fault—I felt unworthy because I must have *been* unworthy. But now it was starting to make sense. I had been wounded. Deeply, deeply wounded. And I never addressed the wound.

Your story is probably different from mine. You may not have been adopted, but you most likely have your own heart-wrenching story. (And if you were adopted, I see you.)

Maybe you remember a moment in your life when everything changed and your innocence was shattered and you had to grow up too fast. Maybe you spent years begging for someone to just see you, hold you, or love you. Maybe the people who were supposed to love you the most made you feel like you were a burden to them—and you took them at their word. Maybe you tried your hardest in school, but your struggle was interpreted as laziness. Maybe your teachers' negative comments are still echoing in the back of your mind. Maybe your parents set impossible standards for you, and no matter how hard you tried, you just couldn't meet them. Maybe you were the only Black kid in your class, and your peers and teachers reminded you of it every single day. Maybe you ate lunch alone in the cafeteria because you didn't fit in. Maybe an abusive relationship stripped you of your worth and dignity.

Whatever your story, you probably received the message at some point, from someone or something, that *you are not worthy*. And you have been living your life trying to prove yourself worthy ever since.

If you're anything like me, you don't have just one story that contributed to the belief in your unworthiness. Most of us have more than one moment, more than one story, that has filled our unworthiness bucket.

But the thing you may not realize is that these messages were not just the results of isolated incidents or exclusive to the person(s) in your life who hurt you. They were rooted in something much deeper than an individual experience. I want to help you uncover the truth about how white supremacy culture is a primary source of the unworthiness we feel. By dismantling those lies, we can reclaim the liberation that we are worthy of living every single day. But more on that later.

Uncovering Primal Wounds

I was sobbing again. I was twenty-two and fresh out of college. The grief would come to me in waves. It was as if the experiences of my entire life had caught up to me in just a few short months. The grief felt so foreign yet so familiar at the same time. Emotions washed over me that no words could adequately describe. What was left were streams of hot, salty tears, gasps for air, and a deep ache to fill the void that had been familiar since my earliest memories.

Desperate for an explanation for my tears, I frantically googled to find "adoptee support" in my local area. I couldn't ignore the trauma any longer. I found an adult adoptee support group that met biweekly on Thursday evenings. The location was about a forty-five-minute Metro ride from where I lived, but I knew I had to be there. I needed answers. I was desperate.

I only made it to one group session, but that was enough to tell me almost everything I needed to know: I had to stop ignoring my trauma.

Being ripped away from my biological mother opened a primal wound the moment my newborn body was not reunited with hers, and that primal wound was still oozing twenty-two years later, after years of neglect and zero attempts to heal it.

The primal wound theory holds that "severing the connection between the infant and biological mother [through adoption] causes a primal wound which often manifests in a sense of loss (depression), basic mistrust (anxiety), emotional and/or behavioral problems and difficulties in relationships with significant others . . . affect[ing] the adoptee's sense of self, self-esteem and self-worth throughout life."[3]

I learned about the concept of the primal wound during that meeting, and every single dot finally connected. When I first looked at those adoption papers when I was sixteen, I realized there was pain and trauma surrounding my birth, as well as my infant and toddler years, and I realized the trauma was having a negative impact on the way I viewed myself and how I believed everyone else viewed me. The night of the adoption meeting, six years later, I was finally able to put a concrete definition *to* the trauma I had experienced. I had uncovered the root of all of my pain. Unbeknownst to me, I had been digging for this root all my life, but inconsistently. I'd start digging a bit, get frustrated and put the shovel down, and continue doing what I did best: ignoring the oozing wound and only picking the shovel back up when I could no longer outrun the pain. That night, my shovel finally hit the root. And I realized it was the root I had been searching for all along.

Adoption is often portrayed as a miracle story. *They all lived happily ever after. Adoption saved this child's life and all is well.* Except all is *not* well. The lost connection between a mother and child is not the same as losing a sock, yet we are often conditioned to treat it that way. You cannot buy a replacement maternal connection like you can buy another sock. If a family chooses to adopt a child, the trauma the child has experienced must be handled with the utmost care. Yet adoption trauma, like most other trauma, is often labeled as shameful and swept under the rug.

I can't speak for every adoptee and adoptive family, but the majority of us have very similar stories. The trauma that was left by our primal wound, in combination with insufficient support and knowledge about what we were enduring internally, has led to a lifetime of deconstructing false beliefs about ourselves and healing the wounds we did not inflict but often feel like we caused. My own daily childhood battle with my unresolved adoption trauma left me feeling ashamed, unworthy, and even suicidal at times.

I lived my life through the filter of this trauma. Anytime I made a mistake, I feared my adoptive mother would stop loving me. When kids at school rejected my friendship, the PTSD from the abandonment I had experienced at birth sent me down a spiral of self-hatred, a place I camped out in for most of my life. When I began to be interested in romantic relationships, I settled for anyone who would show me an ounce of attention, because I was desperate to feel like I was worthy of love. *Oh look, evidence of the primal wound theory in real life!*

It astonishes me that the evidence of my trauma was so blatantly obvious yet ignored for so long. The red lights had been flashing for quite some time. But often when you're knee-deep in such trauma, you can't see it—especially when you're a child, which is why much of childhood trauma is not dealt with, which further complicates the lasting physical and mental damage childhood trauma causes. Data shows us that unresolved childhood trauma increases one's likelihood of struggling with alcoholism, biological and/or neurological disorders, chronic depression and/or anxiety disorders, substance use disorder, suicide, and more.[4]

I was unaware of my trauma during those tender childhood years, but I knew how tumultuous I felt inside whenever someone told me how lucky I was to be adopted. I didn't dare to express that I felt the exact opposite of lucky. I didn't dare share that I frequently grieved the loss of a woman I had never met. I didn't dare admit how depressed I felt and how often I questioned whether I belonged on this earth. So, as many adoptees do, I suppressed my anguish, put a smile on my face, nodded, and said, "I sure am."

———

While the primal wound theory specifically pertains to adoption, I believe the concept can be transferred to most of us, regardless of our origin stories. Let's break this phrase down and define both words separately. *Primal* is defined as "relating to an early stage in evolutionary development; primeval," as well as "essential; fundamental."[5] *Wound* is either a physical injury or "an injury to someone's feelings or reputation."[6] When you put these definitions together outside of the context of adoption, a primal wound can be experienced by anyone who has endured trauma during their early years. And unfortunately, I don't think any of us is exempt from this affliction. Are we all aware of our primal wounds? That's a different story.

Whether we know it or not, our primal wounds have been busy serving as the filter from which we navigate life since the moment they were inflicted upon us. They affect how we handle every interaction, perceive every encounter, and make every decision. They are the blueprint from which we build our lives, even though most of us have no idea that we're using a blueprint to begin with.

Hold on to the revelations you are having right now. You're going to need them in just a bit.

The Primal Wound of a Nation

Adoption was my original traumatic event that laid the foundation for how I navigated every corner of my life. The longer I went without working to heal and reverse its effects, the longer I spent building a structure that allowed the repercussions of that trauma to lay a foundation and erect large pillars in my life.

In a similar way, our society has ignored and denied the traumatic truth of our nation's founding cataclysm and its aftermath.

We have been taught that our society is *perfect*. We are the land of the free and the home of the brave! Our nation was founded on ideals and principles that promise freedom for every human being. Right? Well, even if you were taught the most whitewashed version of our nation's history, you probably know that freedom was not a reality for all human beings when America was founded. And much like the way an adopted child is told to gloss over their primal trauma, we are taught to move on from the "imperfections" of our country's racist "past." We are taught to believe that once Martin Luther King Jr. gave his "I Have a Dream" speech on the steps of the Lincoln Memorial, all Americans were free and generations of state-sanctioned trauma and inequality were instantly healed.

In reality, we as a nation (and Western society as a whole) have failed to discern how the entire structure of our country was built on the foundation of creating a system that benefitted a specific type of person (wealthy white men) through colonization, chattel slavery, and capitalism. And those three Cs are based on the premise of white supremacy. Society wants us to downplay the reality of our nation's primal wound while simultaneously convincing us that any lasting effects are just our imagination. What we are left with is a population of humans who are walking through a cloud of normalized trauma that isn't our fault while fully shouldering the blame for it.

Our society's warning lights are worn out from flashing.

We are desperate. We are a desperate society filled with people who feel unworthy of life, love, and true liberation, and that is because societal structures and standards that were constructed from our nation's founding have led us to believe that we are not enough.

If we don't hold our society accountable, it will never change. The next generation will be left to deal with these unhealed wounds while society continues to perpetuate deeper injury, dispensing only small Band-Aids and no true healing.

Trauma cannot be ignored. Period. Yet, our society loves to show an ignorant neutrality toward the imprint of our nation's initial wound, which only serves to perpetuate that wound, because there is a deep desire to hold on to the hierarchical systems it created as a result. So society chooses to blindfold itself and pretend it cannot see the harm the construction of white supremacy has caused. This has allowed for the foundation of white supremacy to evolve into a white supremacy culture. The more we continue to pretend this wound does not exist, the more it spreads and the deeper it gets. Just like with our own individual primal wounds.

We must take the blindfold off. This is the only way we can start to heal. We don't have room for neutrality. We don't have time for further ignorance. Reclaiming our enoughness depends on us becoming aware of the structures and systems that have been constructed for our oppression. Our collective humanity is at stake.

The wound of white supremacy created the disease of white supremacy culture that has led you to believe that you are not enough. This system in which we all reside created unwritten rules that have convinced you that your humanity is conditional upon following those rules. I'd even go as far as to say that white supremacy and its culture are *directly linked to your own trauma,* no matter what it is.

Getting to the Roots of Our Wounds

Like most adoptions, my adoption wasn't an isolated incident but rather the result of a deeply broken child welfare and foster care system. This doesn't mean that adoption can't be beautiful, meaningful, and even necessary. But have you ever stopped to think about what causes a child to need to be placed for adoption in the first place? What events, systems, and structures make a mother and father unable to care for their child? How have we normalized and ignored the trauma of adoption in the name of self-centered saviorism?

The roots are found in white supremacy. Just take a look at these disparities within the foster care system:

- While Black children only make up 13.71 percent of the population, they make up 22.75 percent of children in foster care.
- American Indian/Alaska Native children account for less than 1 percent of the population, yet they account for 2.4 percent of children in foster care.
- White children represent 50.5 percent of the population, yet they represent only 44.37 percent of children in foster care.[7]

These numbers are not a coincidence. These data points don't exist because communities of color collectively make inferior parenting choices at higher rates than white families. That may be what society has hinted at—or even straight up told you, depending on your upbringing—but it's just not true. These statistics are joined by many others that prove the realities of systemic racism, which is the primary weapon our society uses to uphold white supremacy. These statistics also directly mirror the poverty disproportionalities within our society, and poverty is the number one reason children enter foster care. Again, these disproportionalities don't exist because communities of color just can't seem to "get it together" or "work harder to get a better job." They exist because our society placed systemic barriers on communities of color that enforced higher numbers of poverty so that the socioeconomic hierarchy would serve as a tangible data point to back up the racial hierarchy our country was founded upon. When you combine these systemic barriers with the subconscious (and conscious) bias toward Black families that leads to Black families and other families of color being investigated at higher rates by Child Protective Services, you are met with the perfect equation for overrepresentation of BIPOC families within the child welfare system.[8] And please understand: none of this is by accident. None of it.

Remember those adoption papers with very little information? Well, there was enough written on them to help me paint a picture of my circumstances and fill in the blanks with conclusions I drew in my imagination. My biological mother was a Hispanic woman (according to the paperwork). What ethnicity, specifically? That was left out. Regardless, she was a Hispanic woman who was intellectually disabled (formerly known as mentally retarded in the '90s) and a ward of the state. She lived in a home with other intellectually disabled adults that was located in a lower income area of Harlem, NYC. My biological father was African American, also intellectually disabled, and from what I understand, in and out of homelessness. Both of my biological parents had a history of alcohol and substance use disorder in their immediate families, neither of them had a formal education, and Child Protective Services had already signed the dotted line for my removal immediately upon my birth.

You can imagine the circumstances beyond their control that led them to having their baby ripped from their arms in the delivery room. I often wonder how life could have been if my biological parents weren't born into a world that predetermined their fate because of their racial, socioeconomic, and disabled identities. But mostly, I grieve for the life they never got a chance to live. I grieve for all that white supremacy stole from them. I grieve for that fateful day—April 11, 1990—where their lives and mine forever changed.

Systemic white supremacy led to the circumstances surrounding the traumatic event of my birth and adoption, which led me to spend my early life believing there was no possible way I was worth anything as a human being. The culture of white supremacy deepened that trauma, convincing me that the only thing I could do to prove my worth was follow society's rules of achievement and perfection. It also made me feel totally crazy for being affected by the separation from my biological mother and placed into a family that was not (originally) my own. It's all connected.

(Please understand: this is not a slight toward my adoptive family. I love my family. They are my rock, and without them I could not stand. The existence of love within your adoptive family does not negate the trauma surrounding adoption and the tragic events that led to that adoption. Two things can be true.)

I won't pretend to know your story, but I want you to know that your deepest emotions are safe with me. You are safe.

Before we go any further, know that you *are* enough. You are more than enough. However, *you* must believe that you are enough, which means you need to heal. I cannot tell you exactly how to heal, but this book can be a crucial step in your healing if you allow it to be. Once we take off our universal blindfolds, look white supremacy squarely in the face, and confront it for what it really is (a socially constructed lie of dehumanization), healing can begin.

If you have grown up believing that you are a burden, it is because you live in a society that loves to minimize anything that isn't connected to achievement, leading you to believe that asking for help is a weakness, thus neglecting your needs. If you struggle with body image, it's because you live in a society that tells you there is only one standard of beauty and you are unworthy if you don't meet that standard. If you were taught that you had to pursue perfection in all you do, it is because society glorifies success over humanity. If you have suffered from abuse silently, it is because society has not created a safe place for you to be heard, often offering protection and excuses for abusers instead of victims. And you may even be able to trace other points of trauma in your life to systemic pitfalls brought about by the structure of our society. If you're not quite there yet, you'll be able to connect more dots as this book progresses.

With each chapter, we will dig deeper. Questions may be popping up for you right now, but resist the urge to get ahead of yourself. Jot them in your journal and then release them for now. Then turn to a fresh page. Think about your own story and what lies you have believed about yourself that have caused you to feel unworthy. I want you to confront those stories to the best of your ability. Your journal is your best friend. If you see a therapist, bring these stories up during your next session. If you're reading this book with a friend, make a coffee date to chat about this first chapter and share your stories with one another.

We will be confronting many of the lies the structures and practices of our Western society have told us. Together we will deconstruct them piece by piece so we can reclaim the liberation that rightly belongs to us.

Grab your journal, and I'll meet you in chapter 2.

Journal Prompts

1. What was my primal wound?
2. How has my primal wound led me to believe the lie that I am not good enough or am unworthy?
3. How will I devote myself to showing up as I read this book, fully committing to breaking up with white supremacy and owning my healing?

2

They Didn't Know Better

"No more than four social outings a month," my mother said as she handed me a handwritten list of clear rules I had to follow without question. "This includes your speech tournaments," she added matter-of-factly.

Ohhhhhkay. This includes my speech tournaments? I was confused before I was even frustrated. What had I done to warrant such drastic measures? I hadn't engaged in any of the typical teenage behavior that would usually prompt such a punitive parental response. In fact, I was actually a pretty good kid. I had zero interest in getting into trouble. I played varsity tennis, participated in competitive speech, starred in leading roles in several high school plays, played in the marching band, and held a part-time job at Dairy Queen—to name just a few of my activities. (I was the best Blizzard maker, by the way. I always gave my customers an extra scoop of cookie dough.)

I was *that* kid: the overachiever. Miss Sign-me-up-for-everything-so-I-can-feel-super-accomplished-and-worthy. You can add to that long, hyphenated name: Also-so-I-can-mask-all-of-my-pain-because-I-feel-broken-inside.

That was the truth. I was absolutely broken inside. I had been for a long time. Years of feeling unworthy had piled on top of one another. By now, I had learned that the better I performed and the more achievements I earned, the more I would receive the actions of being loved, praised, and valued I was so desperately seeking. Therefore, I added as many activities to my schedule as I could, hoping my accomplishments would garner the affection my vulnerable heart longed for. Also, so I could keep busy. Keeping busy was how I medicated my depression, though I didn't realize that was what I was doing.

My story is not unique. Many parents and guardians have a history of speaking the languages of achievement and perfectionism with their children. One of the numerous reasons many of us walk around with a belief that we are not good enough is due to receiving impossibly high standards from our parents. Obviously, this isn't everyone's story, but it's a common one. Such standards have been normalized and justified for generations. The idolatry of the American Dream and the false promise that an individualistic and perfectionistic work ethic will get you there are just a *few* of the societal beliefs that have played a role in this justification.

If we dig deeper, the real roots of perfectionism have one name: *whiteness*. Whiteness, which manifests as racism, ableism, classism, and sexism. Whiteness has told us that there is only one right way to be successful in our society, and it looks and sounds like a white, able-bodied, cisgendered male who graduated from an elite Ivy League school. The driving force behind our society, whiteness says, *If you don't fit my standards, there is no room for you here.*

If you're already white, then whiteness is your ticket to the life, liberty, and pursuit of happiness our society promises. As long as you strive for perfection, you're good to go. What no one will tell you, however, is that perfect whiteness is impossible to achieve. The standards have continued to rise throughout the generations and have left every single one of us panting in exhaustion from the chase.

Now, if you're BIPOC, it has never really been about the American Dream or that grand pursuit of happiness. For us, perfectionism is key to our *survival*.

If there was one lesson I took away from my childhood, it was this: *As a Black woman, you will have to work twice as hard and achieve twice as much just to get half as far as white people.* This message was drilled into me to the point that it almost became my identity. I am Black, so I must prove myself in everything I do. I must prove I am intelligent. I must prove I'm not a criminal and I deserve to be here. I must prove I am just as good as my white counterparts.

This was my reality and I had (mostly) accepted it. What other choice did I have? As my mom used to say, "It's all about how you play their game." I could either sink or swim, and playing their game was how I had to swim. We set high standards and expected achievement of those standards because that was the only way to guarantee my survival, let alone my success in this world.

So, insert the high standards. Insert the demands of perfection. Anything less than perfect, or at least near-perfect, was not welcome. By the time I was in high school, I had a very strategic formula for success I was expected to follow:

- C's are not allowed.
- B's should be A's.
- You must take honors classes.
- You must be involved in extracurricular activities.
- You must volunteer a certain number of hours every month.
- You must apply for a certain number of college scholarships.

- Any activity that won't get you a college scholarship is a waste of time, even if you love it.
- You may only go on four social outings a month.

The "only four social outings a month" rule was added to my list of demands during the height of competitive speech season. We had tournaments every Saturday from January to April. Just imagine a bunch of somewhat nerdy high school students waking up at the crack of dawn on a freezing Minnesota Saturday morning, putting on a suit more formal than what most adults wore to work, and spending the entire day performing speeches and competing for medals. It sounds like trouble, doesn't it? (If you didn't read that with a hint of sarcasm, do me a favor and reread it. K? Thanks.)

In all seriousness, speech saved my life.

By the time I was a teenager, those internal whispers of feeling like a mistake had severely intensified. My biological mother was never "supposed" to have children. But here I was. Existing, fumbling around, and making endless mistakes in an environment where love was typically displayed the more perfection was achieved. By the time I was fourteen, I hated myself. And the speech team was the miracle God used to save me from myself. I excelled at speech in a way I had never excelled at anything I'd ever done before. It felt almost effortless. It was like I had this unexplainable natural talent that was so clearly tied to whatever purpose God had for me, even though I didn't yet know what that was. It gave me hope. I felt like I was finally given a glimpse of why I may have been placed on this earth after all.

Speech competitions gave me purpose. The speech *team*, however, gave me a family. It was the first time I had ever belonged to a group where I didn't have to prove myself worthy. They were my first group of friends that didn't make me feel like I had to adhere to a certain set of "cool standards" to fit in. They accepted me for everything I was: my quirks, my kinks, my bright orange Chucks, and my broken soul. They even made sure I received an invitation to every team outing, lined up rides for me, and refused to allow me to be a wallflower. I finally belonged somewhere.

Unfortunately, those team outings were short-lived.

Due to the rule.

The four social outings a month including speech tournaments rule.

The rule that knocked the wind out of me, but, if I'm honest, didn't totally surprise me.

Asking my mom's permission to attend anything social always felt a bit like preparing to defend a dissertation. It didn't happen often, since I was always a bit of a loner, but when I did desire to socialize, I had to come prepared with a list of reasons why I felt I deserved to go. If and when permission was granted, it was usually given reluctantly and with some sort of condition attached to it. Socializing wasn't a human right in our house. It was a privilege that needed to be earned, and usually I hadn't done quite enough to prove myself worthy. There was always a task on the condition checklist I needed to accomplish before the fun permission was granted.

So, when I was handed the infamous list of rules, it was clear I could either go to the speech tournaments themselves or the after-parties, but I couldn't attend both. We both knew that if it came down to the tournament or the after-party, the tournament would always win. There was no way I was giving up those tournaments. There was no way I was giving up the first time I had ever felt true purpose in my life. So, with begrudging frustration, I said good-bye to that feeling of belonging I had spent sixteen years longing for.

This felt like a punch to the gut. Like I had failed another expectation, even though I wasn't quite sure what I had failed, exactly. I didn't know what I had or hadn't done to warrant such exorbitant action. I just knew that the same shameful beliefs from childhood came racing back to me.

You're not good enough.

You're not worthy.

See, she doesn't really *love you.*

My mom was completely unaware of the unworthiness battle raging inside of me. I never expected her to know. And I don't blame her for this battle. We are just now coming to terms with the lifelong psychological damage adoptee trauma causes, as more data emerges and more adult adoptees are speaking out about their experiences, so of course we were both unaware of my raging worthiness war back then. And of course, she didn't think that asserting high standards and expecting me to meet them added more ammunition to my internal war. Those high standards were her way of *assuring my survival.* She sought to teach her Black daughter how to navigate a world that was deliberately built on denying success to Black people, especially Black women. She was determined to raise an independent woman who was more than prepared to stay afloat in a world that many drown in. And she successfully did just that. Because of her diligence and discipline, I entered the world of adulthood as a self-sufficient young woman and have managed to keep my head above water since my emergence into its raging sea. I will forever credit her for instilling a resilience in me that allowed me to conquer every battle that would have otherwise caused imminent peril.

I believe my mom operated from a deep fear instilled by our white-dominant society that tells Black women, as well as everyone else, that despite our best efforts we will never be enough. This fear is so ingrained in each of us that it's invisible, yet it drives our every thought and action. It disguises itself as normalized perfectionism and the idolatry of success. It tricks us into believing that even the slightest amount of rest or fun must be earned, otherwise they are mere distractions and evidence of laziness. It lies to us and tells us we will never be successful or good enough if we dare to slow down, give ourselves grace, and unapologetically accept our imperfections.

Oh, and to do something you truly love just because it brings you joy? Forget about it.

My mother was terrified I wouldn't be successful. Every time she saw me spend time doing anything she believed would take me off the path to success, she panicked. She had been taught you have to earn your worth in this world or, as she used to say, "Earn your keep." So she taught me to earn my keep by primarily showing affection and giving praise after she felt like I deserved it. After I had *earned it*. In her mind, she was teaching me the ways of the world—making sure I would never get comfortable or settle when there was more to prove and more work to be done.

There's Always More to the Story

Our toxic white supremacist and patriarchal society breeds normalized cultural characteristics such as perfectionism, individualism, and a false belief that progress is only achieved by striving for more. We're taught to believe these are the keys to either success or survival, depending on which societal position you occupy. Many of our parents, driven by urgency and fear from white supremacy culture, desperately instilled these characteristics in us, which were then reaffirmed by society.

Our capitalist, anti-Black, anti-woman, and anti-everything-else-that-is-not-a-rich-white-male society has deceived all of us into believing that we must spend our entire lives chasing success to prove our worth. As children, we are taught to be strong, to toughen up, to never let them see us sweat. We are taught that love is conditional upon our obedience and infallibility instead of being taught that it is our weaknesses that make our humanity all the more beautiful. Then, as we become adults, we are left with open wounds of inadequacy and worthlessness that feel impossible to heal.

Until very recently, if I had told you this story about my mom— the limited social outings, high standards, and other childhood experiences that negatively impacted my self-worth—I would have still believed that her parenting choices were an intentional result of what I believed to be her disdain for me. Surely my inability to be what my mother expected me to be was the reason she felt the need to choose tough love rather than unconditional affection. I wouldn't have wondered what actually drove my mother to believe that high standards and restriction were the best ways to parent me. I wouldn't have considered her own story, how she may not have received the expression of love she needed as a child either, and the way society wrote the narrative that she, and every other Black girl like her, would never be good enough for this white man's world.

Of course my mom parented me the way she did! What choice did she have?

The heart-wrenching reality is that this type of childhood trauma is so common we may not recognize it as traumatic. I used to believe my story was novel—that I was the only one who received intermittent affection, who felt like they were never good enough, or who felt like a burden to their parents. The unfortunate truth is, those who haven't experienced some level of childhood trauma are exceptions to the rule.

Perfectionism and unachievable standards aren't the only criteria for childhood trauma that can lead us to feel unworthy. You may be able to relate to every single word in my story, or you may have had a very different experience. Perhaps you heard only negative comments about your physical appearance because your parents believed wholeheartedly in the fatphobic propaganda that a thin body was a superior body, so you learned to attach your worth to what you saw in the mirror. Maybe your parents were raised to the standard that children were to be seen and not heard, so when it was their turn to parent, they demanded silent submission and downplayed your humanity, and now you struggle with demanding to be seen, heard, and valued as an adult. Maybe you have a story of agonizing abuse, neglect, or loss that sought to strip you of your worth, and you've barely begun to put those pieces back together. No matter your story, chances are that your unworthiness bucket began to fill up during childhood.

But now it's time to pour it out.

(*Disclaimer: Before I continue, I want you to know that if you experienced any forms of serious abuse or neglect during your childhood, I see you and I am holding space for you. This chapter is not here to make an excuse for how you were mistreated or to downplay your circumstances. I understand that there is no way I could ever know everyone's story or the depths of your pain.*)

Look Beyond the Person

To begin healing our wounds of unworthiness and take back our power, we must dig deep and see the roots of this pain for what it really is. The truth is, our culture has been feeding us the lie of unworthiness in every aspect of our lives. For most of us, this lie took root during childhood because our parents or guardians were unwittingly influenced by white supremacy and white supremacy culture. The point is not to place blame here but to see exactly how the trauma we've endured shares the same roots.

Parents and guardians who demanded perfection did so because they were taught it was the only way to succeed or survive in our society. Maybe their outlook was shaped by growing up in poverty or experiencing food insecurity. Or, maybe they came from a long line of Ivy League degree-earners, and they faced immense pressure to live up to the family name. Parents who tied your value to your physical appearance were taught by our society's white-washed beauty standards that this is where value lies. Maybe they faced discrimination for how they looked when they sought job opportunities, or maybe their parents, brainwashed by fatphobic advertising, shamed their eating habits from a young age. Parents who were dismissive toward you may have been so because their parents, and society as a whole, have been dismissive toward them. Heartbreaking stories of abuse and neglect have their own roots in white supremacy, whether due to our broken capitalist systems, toxic patriarchy and misogyny, or strongholds of generational abuse.

White supremacy culture places perfectionism, objectivity, individualism, paternalism, power, and more on a pedestal and demands these traits from us in order for us to be accepted and valued. (You'll learn more about these specific traits in chapter 3.) We are measured only by what we can produce, and we are only given the full opportunity to do so if our appearance and behavior live up to the ideals of whiteness. This is why our parents trained us to live up to those ideals, regardless of the harm caused by the ideals themselves and the way they instilled them. Unless by some slim chance your family figured out society's true agenda, this was likely the way they were taught to approach life in order to have a fighting chance at success.

The systems and structures of our society determine who can be successful, free, and happy. Even those who can access these benefits often have to uphold toxic practices to prove that they're deserving. This is the inescapable foundation of our society that drives everything we do. It has continued to build and grow with each new generation, adding more salt to our collective wound. If we don't stop it, we will continue to perpetuate it. We run the risk of passing on the very trauma we have endured to future generations without even realizing what we are doing.

For us to heal, to reclaim our worth, we must not only dig deep enough to discover the roots of our collective feelings of unworthiness but also dig deep enough to pull them all out *together*.

That starts with confronting your childhood and getting honest about the trauma you endured, then looking beyond the person(s) who was the deliverer of that trauma. We must see past our parents and guardians to the constant driving force of our white supremacist society that caused them to believe what they believed, to feel the way they felt, and to behave the way they behaved. If our view of self-worth is distorted, we must understand that our parents' or guardians' view of their self-worth was likely distorted too.

My father helped me see my mother as a human. A human with pain, sorrow, fears, and secret dreams that were never realized. A human who, just like every single one of us, deeply desires to be seen, heard, and loved unconditionally. A human who became a mother and, like every other mother, put temporary Band-Aids over life's battle scars in order to show up the best way she knew how for her kid. Seeing my mother like this also gave me permission to see myself as a human, and I think the more I allowed myself to be a human, the more I gave my mother permission to let her humanity show too.

My mom and I call each other almost every day. We laugh together and continue growing in our shared love of music and shopping, and her grandchildren squeal with delight when she answers their FaceTime calls. With every conversation we have, more humanity is revealed and more healing occurs. Humanity is what was missing all along. And humanity is what our culture of white supremacy steals from us, taking our self-worth right along with it. When you don't see yourself as a human being, it impedes your ability to see others as human beings too. When you don't see yourself as worthy, it is nearly impossible to honor the worth and value of others. Even those you love with all your heart. Even your children.

I know it's painful. You may be in a place similar to the one I was in a few years ago when I couldn't see beyond the people who caused me pain. That's understandable. This is a journey, and we're on it together.

I want to make it clear that I do not have all the answers for your healing. Instead, I am inviting you to heal right along with me. I'm opening up my journey to you, in hopes that a part of my journey will help you with your own.

Now I want you to reflect on your childhood. You can use the following journal prompts to guide you. Think specifically about your childhood and write about your experience and your parents' story. If you can, ask your parents about their childhoods and what they were taught. See if you can draw some connections between their childhood beliefs and your own. If it's not too painful, try to see your parents as human beings who were just doing the best they could, given their beliefs and their trauma.

Then forgive them. And forgive yourself. You did your best, and so did they. It sucks, and it's painful, but you can heal.

You can heal.

Journal Prompts

1. What are the various traumas I endured during my childhood? (The size of the trauma is irrelevant. Small, large . . . it all matters.)

2. How did the behaviors and actions of those who raised me form the way I viewed myself?

3. From what I know about the adults who raised me, what do I think may have influenced their behaviors, actions, and decisions, even though those actions may have caused me pain?

4. What parts of my parents' story (or the story of the adults who raised me) have I not considered until now?

5. In what ways do I think society impacted how the adults who raised me viewed the world? In what ways did those viewpoints affect how they raised me?

6. Am I in a place to forgive those who hurt me in my childhood? Am I in a place to see beyond their actions and look deeply into their stories, their perspectives, and their own pain they may have been going through? If yes, how can I do so? If I'm not ready yet, what are my next steps?

3

Never Enough

White supremacy culture.

Let's be real—this is the elephant in the room. The big old smelly elephant in the room. (Um, okay, I kind of feel like I should apologize to all elephants right now. I didn't need to play them like that.)

For the last two chapters, I've slowly introduced you to the premise that **white supremacy culture is the root of our entire society's collective battle with unworthiness.** This is a bold statement, to say the least, yet I know at my core it's true. Once you see it, you can't unsee it. And once you can't unsee it, you can't help but make it part of your life's work to join in the fight to dismantle the system that has led us here in the first place. But let's not get ahead of ourselves. First, we must clearly see just how white supremacy culture has gotten us to where we are today. Like I've said before, our freedom from the impossible standards depends on this. Our souls are so desperate to be free.

But before we get started, can I be honest with you real quick? I wrestle internally about using the phrases *white supremacy* and *white supremacy culture.* I understand that many people wish there were other phrases that felt more "neutral" to explain these systemic problems. I understand that these words can be quite a turnoff to many and are loaded with all kinds of baggage. We've been taught that white supremacy is represented in only three things: white men in Klan hoods, violent lynchings of Black people during the Jim Crow South, and extremists in self-proclaimed white supremacist groups today. It's only recently that we have begun confronting the truth about white supremacy as the basis for our entire societal structure, and this truth is actively resisted. It ruffles feathers, especially if you identify as white. It can feel like a direct attack on your personhood and your racial/cultural/ethnic identity. You might find yourself feeling defensive; surely you should not have to feel guilty about being white or benefitting from and enjoying the society you were born into.

Even though I am not white, I get it. I've found myself feeling defensive, too, about certain beliefs and behavioral practices I'd put on a pedestal without realizing they were harmful characteristics of white supremacy culture. And as a Black person who exists in a society that has forever treated my culture and identity as wrong, threatening, disgusting, and inferior, I understand just how hurtful it is to feel like the culture you identify with is being attacked. My hope is that this chapter helps you understand that the harm is not in *being white* but in the societal structure that has been constructed out of the belief that to be white is to be *better than* everyone else who is not white and the unhealthy cultural propensities that have stemmed from this core belief.

Now, let's quickly review the definition of white supremacy and white supremacy culture so you don't have to flip back to the prelude (because that's annoying, am I right?).

White supremacy is

[A] political, economic and cultural system in which whites over-
whelmingly control power and material resources, conscious and
unconscious ideas of *white superiority* and *entitlement* are widespread,
and relations of *white dominance* and *non-white subordination* are daily
reenacted across a broad array of institutions and social settings.[1]

We can see the systems of white supremacy at play within our
political power structure and the laws that are created by those in
power, as well as in our education system, our healthcare system, the
corporate system, the media, and, most importantly, our everyday
lives. All we need to do is look at who holds the majority of the
power, influence, wealth, and success within our society, and we
can find clear evidence of white supremacy.

Through the construction of white supremacy, white supremacy
culture emerged as the dominant cultural belief system in our society. Best defined, as mentioned earlier, *white supremacy culture* is the
norms, customs, values, beliefs, and standards that have taught us
that whiteness is better, whiteness is the picture of success, whiteness
is value.[2] Think of white supremacy as the roots and trunk of the
tree and white supremacy culture as the branches and the leaves.
Now, let's be clear—this is not a flourishing tree. This tree is rotten
from the deepest of roots to the tip of each leaf. The lie this culture
tells us is that unless we assimilate ourselves to strive for whiteness,
we will never be enough to benefit from it.

One of the key words I want you to look at in that definition
is *norms*. It's vital to understand that white supremacy culture is
the norm in our society, so the harmful cultural characteristics
that white supremacy culture has produced have also become our
norms. White supremacy culture breeds certain characteristics and

traits that come from living within a system that was built for the sole purpose of creating and protecting elite white "Christian" male dominance and demanding the subordination of all who are non-white, non-elite, non-Christian, non-male, or "other" to uphold that dominance.

Historically, this was done very literally and obviously through overt and legalized racism. Presently, we still see these systems continuing to uphold that racism, albeit more covertly, yet still quite obvious. However, we now have an added layer of elite white dominance that does not look like the wealthy, landowning white males we may be picturing from our history books. The picture has been translated into a very narrow standard that portrays what success, value, and worthiness are within our society, which requires a majority of us to dehumanize ourselves in order to stand a chance to even attempt to meet that standard.

Essentially, society demands assimilation to be considered worthy, and the only way to achieve such assimilation is to embody the unnatural and narrow characteristics that idealized elite white men penned as the markers for success.

Okay, I know you're wondering when I'm going to tell you what these characteristics of white supremacy culture are. Don't worry, I've got you. But first, some clarification. This list of characteristics was put together by Dr. Tema Okun with the organization Dismantling Racism Works.[3] Dr. Okun and other scholars at Dismantling Racism Works have updated this list of characteristics throughout the years as their research has expanded, but the underlying theme always remains: we've normalized believing that we aren't good enough unless we fit into this narrow box defined by the white men who created our society to ensure worldly white dominance, and that process is killing us.

Another disclaimer: as the book continues, you will learn more about why these characteristics are considered standards of *white-*

ness. However, this doesn't mean they only describe white people and are only natural to white people or that non-white people are incapable of possessing these traits, nor does it mean all white people possess all of these traits. These characteristics are considered part of the standard of whiteness in our society because white people created the systems that bred them. Most of these characteristics are in opposition to the cultural norms of Indigenous, African/Black, non–Westernized European, and other non-white cultures, because those cultures tend to focus more on collective community rather than power, profit, and individualism.

Since the value system created by white men hungry for power and desperate to maintain white superiority is the dominant value system of our society, the resulting characteristics have become associated with *whiteness*. They are:

- Fear
- Perfectionism
- One right way
- Paternalism
- Objectivity
- Qualified
- Binary or either/or thinking
- Denial
- Defensiveness
- Right to comfort
- Fear of conflict
- Individualism
- Power hoarding
- Progress is more

- Quantity over quality
- Worship of the written word
- Urgency[4]

We will refer back to this list throughout the book.

It is important to know that all of these characteristics have been so normalized in our society that we barely notice them, let alone the harm they cause. If we *are* able to see the faults of these characteristics, we will usually blame those faults on ourselves rather than seeing their effects as systemic issues. We can thank the individualistic nature white supremacy culture has "gifted us" for that one.

Perfectionism, for example, is arguably one of the most recognizable characteristics of white supremacy culture in our society. It has become an expectation to exude at least some level of perfectionism, and if you don't identify with any level of it, you've probably felt as if you were a bit of an outlier at times. We have been taught that our value lies in overachieving, being as productive as possible, and doing everything perfectly. And if we don't prioritize these characteristics within ourselves, we are expected to feel shame. The praise and reward we receive from society when we "go the extra mile" to achieve "by any means necessary" contribute to the shame we feel should we ever want to choose humanity over productivity.

Here's the thing, though: we are humans, not robots. We aren't natural-born perfectionists or overachievers to the degree we are expected to perform within society. We are forcing ourselves to behave in a way that is unnatural and inhuman.

We have normalized and praised perfectionism so much that we have become oblivious to its toxicity. And if we *can* see that toxicity, we find a way to blame ourselves rather than blaming perfectionism or the societal pressures that cause perfectionism. We begin to burn out, our relationships suffer, our health deteriorates, and yet somehow we think that the answer to this problem is . . . more perfectionism. Obviously, if we are suffering we just need to "try harder," right? We think we just need to perfect that routine, get up earlier, work out more, drink more green smoothies, make more money, and find a better day planner and somehow, the burnout flames will magically extinguish.

This is how white supremacy culture works. It lies to you by telling you that your shortcomings are entirely your fault and that you just need to push yourself more, work harder, and do better until you are finally good enough.

(Spoiler alert: according to white supremacy culture, you will never be good enough. Another spoiler alert: white supremacy culture is made up and can be dismantled. And you are already good enough.)

Let's get one thing clear before we continue: I am not advocating we abandon accountability, owning our shortcomings, or pursuing excellence. These are all good things. However, if your measuring stick of success is the one white supremacy culture handed to you, you will forever be stuck on the hamster wheel of chasing impossible perfectionism that brings about suffering and burnout that you believe is . . . you guessed it . . . normal.

Normal does not mean right. Read that again.

White supremacy culture, and all of the characteristics that come with it, is our norm, but it is *not* right. It only feels right because it is all we know. Again, it is our cultural DNA, and it can feel very weird to challenge that. Kind of like you're challenging your own identity. If you are feeling conflicting emotions right now, that is justifiable. Allow yourself to go through the range of emotions you may be experiencing as you go through this process. It's all part of the journey, and every second of it is more than worth it.

To fully comprehend all of this, we must ask ourselves, How did we get here? Cliché, I know, but true. We can't move forward without accurately looking at how history has shaped exactly how we got where we are right now. The good news is that I've done all the hard work for you. All you have to do is keep reading.

The Creation of Race, Whiteness, and the Lie of White Superiority

There is no such thing as a superior race, religion, ethnicity, culture, or any other identity. (Yes, I said religion.) Yet there is a particular dichotomy that has been forged throughout Western history: white is superior and everyone else is inferior. But how did we get here? How was this idea created in the first place, and *why* was it created?

I'm going to give you a crash course in modern history. This will be an overview, so if there is anything you find particularly interesting that you want to learn more about, I encourage you to research those topics further at your convenience. My goal here is for you to have a firm grasp on the development of white supremacy, its evolution through history, and how it created the *culture* of white supremacy that currently has a vicious stronghold on our modern society.

Climate Theory, Colonization, and the Beginnings of Anti-Blackness

There wasn't always a white race. If you would have asked a European person what their ethnicity, or identity, was any time prior to the mid-seventeenth century, they would have answered with their country of origin and their religious affiliation (for example, English Protestant or Irish Catholic). Being *white* wasn't a thing back then. However, superiority beliefs most certainly were a thing. Having a superiority complex, among many other issues of the heart, has been a human problem since the fall of humankind. Before the creation of race, these superiority beliefs were based on religion, culture, and even climate.[5]

I remember taking a world philosophy course my senior year of high school. I'm sure I learned something about Greek philosopher Aristotle, but I cannot for the life of me remember learning about his climate theory for human hierarchy. I'm certain that if I did learn about it back then, it was probably an uncomfortable idea for me to sit with as a seventeen-year-old girl well aware of her Blackness in a predominantly white high school. Perhaps that's why I blocked that lesson out? Who knows.

Anyway, according to Aristotle's *Politics*, extremely hot and extremely cold climates produced intellectually, physically, and morally inferior human beings. The Greeks, located in a rather temperate climate, were considered by Aristotle to be superior simply because of their location and the way their skin looked as a result of that location. To the degree that your skin was either fairer or darker than Greek norms, you were not only considered uglier but also more unintelligent, weaker, and more barbaric.[6] For example, a super pale face indicated that you didn't get outdoors much, which the Greeks believed to be moronic. The lack of sunlight contributed to the lack of intelligence they believed those individuals to have. On the other hand, if you were extremely dark, you were considered a "burnt face" and thought to live a savage lifestyle.[7]

These axioms allowed the Greeks to justify enslaving both Africans and Eastern Europeans (Slavs). At the start of the Common Era, or after Christ was born, the Romans also justified their slave-holding practices using Aristotle's climate theory. It was often stated that the climate theory was God ordained.[8] Some humans were just born to be masters and some were just born to be enslaved. Even though there were scholars in antiquity that fought these dehumanizing beliefs, just as social justice activists are fighting for equality today, the dogma that God divinely ordained the enslavement of "morally inferior humans" prevailed.

Climate theory didn't start and end in antiquity. It helped lay the foundation for the racist ideas we know today: white is right and Black is not. As the Common Era progressed, the enslavement of sub-Saharan Africans increased while the enslavement of Eastern European Slavs decreased. The Slavic communities began to protect themselves from capture by building forts and hiding out from slave raiders.[9]

Meanwhile, the riches that were known to be in sub-Saharan Africa were fought over between Western European Christians and North African Muslims. The Muslim regions in Northern Africa assisted the Western Europeans with the enslavement of sub-Saharan Africans in exchange for access to their lucrative gold and salt supply.[10] But the Portuguese didn't like going through these Islamic middlemen, so they figured they would go down the coast of West Africa and seek out the goods for themselves while capturing and enslaving some Africans while they were at it.[11]

It's important to note that in the eyes of the Portuguese, this was considered missionary work. *Christian* missionary work. Missionary work that claimed to "save" the barbaric Africans who were in "desperate need" of "religious and civil salvation."[12]

If you ever wondered what marked the difference between enslavement before the transatlantic slave trade and enslavement after the start of the transatlantic slave trade, the answer is simple: Portugal.

Their determination to find and enslave Africans for themselves was one thing, but their documentation of their slaveholding practices and the way they wrote about the livelihood of Africans is what changed the game for everyone. They not only recorded their slaveholding practices so that other Europeans could learn from them but also made sure to document what they believed to be true about Africans, their customs, and why they were indeed lesser human beings (read: heathen, behemoth, ugly, inferior, only existing for the purpose of enslavement, not really human).[13] They recorded it all in a book entitled *The Chronicle of the Discovery and Conquest of Guinea*, and then they spread it like wildfire. This book gave the entire Western world permission to view Africans as subhuman, capture them, torture them, enslave them, and use them solely for capital gain and white supremacy, while convincing themselves that since it was God's divine assignment for them, it was justified.[14] This was the beginning of the racist ideas that sculpted our modern world.

As time marched on, "inferior" humans went from being both extremely pale and extremely dark humans to only the dark humans. And, as European Christians took over the slave trade, the Christian belief of religious and cultural superiority became the primary justifier of not only enslavement but the entirety of European colonization. By the mid-fifteenth century, Christians believed that their faith in God granted them dominion over the earth and entitlement to whatever resources, land, people, and wealth they desired.[15]

Do you remember learning about European colonialism? More than likely, you were taught that colonialism was simply about exploration and discovery. It was innocent and pure. The settlers were just fulfilling their "manifest destiny," right? By the time I learned these concepts in school, I had already been conditioned to believe that white people were better than BIPOC and that it "just made sense" that they violently conquered land that "rightfully belonged to them." I didn't have the words to articulate it, but this idea that white people were more civilized than Black and brown people, were smarter than us, and had more resources and power was just something I . . . accepted. I never questioned learning about how white men committed mass genocide to steal land.

Because I had only ever seen white people in leadership positions, my little childhood mind assumed that was just how it was supposed to be. Even though I knew that the violent conquest of Indigenous land and the merciless treatment of enslaved Africans was wrong,

I never questioned the fact that it happened, because I had subconsciously accepted our position in society as second-class citizens.

As Ta-Nehisi Coates, author of *Between the World and Me*, says, "Race is the child of racism, not the father."[16] We have been trained to believe the opposite. For centuries, modern humanity has believed that race was God ordained and scientific. The superiority of the white race and the inferiority of the *other* races is what justified the racism. Black, Indigenous, People of Color deserved the racist treatment they were given because they would never live up to the golden standard that is whiteness. I am so grateful to God that we now know the truth: **racism came first, and race was created as a result of racism.**

I wish I had known this truth as a little girl. As early as age five, I had internalized that I was *less than* because I was Black. And because I was Black, racism was warranted. In that order.

From European to White and the Progression of Enslavement

The more enslavement and the colonization of the Western world grew, the more literature was written to document, justify, and spread the idea that Africans were barbaric, heathenish animals only created for enslavement by white Christians.

According to Kenneth Silverman, author of *The Life and Times of Cotton Mather*, the Puritan Christians believed they had been granted dominion over the earth, wealth, civilization, beauty, and God himself, and it was the Christian's duty to "save" the Africans by way of enslavement.[17] They sought to convert enslaved people to Christianity in order to make them more submissive and humble in their slave duties, preaching a false gospel that obedience to their masters would make them more "white."[18] Historical literature such as *The Negro Christianized* spread the ideology that God actually sent African slaves over to Christian America to learn from the "master's gospel." The more this "slave gospel" was preached, the more Christianity became synonymous with whiteness. Eventually, the two terms blurred into one: white.[19]

Let's pause for a quick disclaimer: mention of the brutal severity and everlasting traumatic impact of American slavery often brings up defensive whataboutisms surrounding Irish and other poor, white indentured servants who performed difficult labor in less-than-ideal conditions during the same period as chattel slavery. Without diving into the deep end of this history, I want to mention something very important: to unite white immigrants of all socioeconomic statuses in the British colonies, lawmakers and slaveholders (planters) created rules and regulations to ensure a marked hierarchical difference between the poorest white person and the Negro slave. There were instances when enslaved people and indentured servants joined together to rebel against their masters and the ruling class. But most of these rebellions failed, and the commonalities between the enslaved and indentured grew strained over things like the creation of laws that gave poor white people special privileges over both enslaved and free Black people.[20]

These privileges purposefully divided poor whites and indentured white servants from enslaved Black people to create a social order that placed Black people at the bottom and white people, no matter their economic class, above them. Throughout history, similar laws have been written to ensure the racial caste system remained in place and white supremacy reigned supreme.

Okay, how you feelin'? I know this is a bit heavy, and you may be thinking, *What does my battle with self-worth have to do with the development of race and racism?*

Don't worry, we're getting there.

Remember, we cannot actively uproot a problem if we cannot find the roots to begin with. In taking a moment to learn this crucial history, you are digging for that root, ensuring that you find the deepest one so you can safely, accurately, and effectively uproot the rotten tree. I want you to remember that while we are learning about the atrocities that, historically, people who have been considered white have committed in the name of Christian superiority, and then later racial superiority, this is not a white people bashing session. These ruthless acts could have been committed by anyone because no one, except Jesus, is above sin.

Most of us know that if we dig even further into antiquity, people groups commonly committed violent and egregious acts against other people groups because of differences in things like religion and a desire for conquest. People have been capturing, invading, and enslaving other people based on the false premise of a superiority complex since the fall of humankind. It has unfortunately been one of the ugliest themes that has transcended the course of humanity, no matter how times have changed.

Living in modern times doesn't make this fact any different. As I'm writing this, in early 2022, President Vladimir Putin of Russia has declared war on Ukraine by way of a deadly, merciless invasion. Why? Because he believes Ukraine belongs to him. As long as humans have inhabited this earth, we have wrestled with this ghastly and sinful idea that somehow we are superior to other humans for whatever reason, and this so-called superiority allows us to steal their rights and privileges at the expense of their humanity. Yet regardless of our religious beliefs, race, ethnicity, gender, class, job, sexual orientation, or what we did last night or last year, no human being is ever better than any other human being.

Every single one of us deserves to exist fully and freely as our whole selves without ever embodying the belief that we aren't good enough just as we are—just as God created us to be. Every single one of us deserves to have equal and equitable access to the earth God gifted us with and to equally participate in the building of a society that values community and love above all else. If we were all truly following the teaching of Jesus, we would be loving our neighbor as Christ first loved us, building that equitable society Jesus fought for, and that would be that.

But, alas, that is not that. And that is why we find ourselves where we are today: living in a society created by the idea that white people and whiteness are superior. Every single moment in Western history, from the minute Africans were deemed an inferior race to the moment you are reading these words, has strategically and intentionally built off the previous one to secure the supremacy of whiteness and white power.

Enslavement led to the creation of the cotton industry, which was America's first Big Business and laid the groundwork for American capitalism. The cotton industry led to the Industrial Revolution, which solidified the goal of white dominance by the Western world that had been set centuries prior. As white-led nations continued to grow their wealth and power over the world, they used this power to set the precedent for how everyone who fell under their influence and control would live their lives.

The Development of White Supremacy (and the Systems That Embolden It)

The Industrial Revolution and the American Dream

Enslavement and colonization were just the beginning of the development of white supremacy and the culture that is its by-product. Together, they built a thoroughly solid foundation that ensured every single pillar, wall, window, and roof built from that foundation strengthened the house of white supremacy so that nothing would ever allow it to crumble. Each decade that followed strategically added to this house.

Toward the end of the nineteenth century, race scientists, who were primarily based in Europe, were busy concocting scientific "theories" to prove the inferiority of Black people. The most widely known is Dr. Samuel Morton's skull theory, which theorized that white people had the largest skulls, indicating the highest level of intelligence.[21] People with Asian ancestry, who were part of the newly created "Mongoloid" race, had medium-sized skulls, so they were of average intelligence. Not as superior as white people, but nowhere close to as inferior as Black people. The "Negroid" race (Black people) were said to have the smallest skulls, which essentially "proved" the climate and religious theories of Black inferiority to be true.[22] Powerful white men now had exactly what they were looking for to not only continue with racism but to use themselves as the measuring stick for intelligence everyone else must live up to. And let's just say . . . they took that power and ran with it.

After the Civil War, enslavement was over and the Industrial Revolution picked up in earnest. The subsequent shift toward a free market ideology created our culture of wealth-chasing capitalism and individualism. (Free market ideology is a market system built on the belief that it is separate from other social institutions, is self-regulating, and operates without bias.)[23] The industrialization of the post–Civil War era brought about new technology from electric light bulbs to gasoline-powered engines, which drastically changed the way the Western world worked and lived. This marked the official end of the village lifestyle humans had relied upon from the moment we came into existence—the lifestyle we were created to live. You know, in community with others, loving and supporting one another, sharing resources, and existing as equals (within our respective villages).

Of course, it is understood that social hierarchies have existed long before the formation of our modern world, but right now, we're talking about how the transition from an agrarian to industrial society resulted in an exponential increase in inequality. Almost overnight, we went from working with the natural rhythms of our humanity and nature to working against them. The invention of electricity allowed laborers to expand their working hours beyond the rise and fall of the sun to a nearly round-the-clock schedule that we still grapple with today. The migration to big cities and transition to factory work shifted society from a collective, village lifestyle to an automated, individualized, work-centered one.[24]

The rich kept getting richer by abusing the labor of those who were beneath them, and the poor kept getting poorer as working and societal conditions grossly deteriorated. And Black people entered into the next phase of our brutal history, the Jim Crow era, which prevented us from having full access to society and the ability to begin building our wealth after two centuries of our wealth and labor being stolen from us.

By the time of the Great Depression, many social critics were already concerned with the repetition, toil, and loss of freedom and autonomy caused by the rapid capitalist growth of the Industrial Revolution.[25] Chasing the possibility of wealth through speculation, moving and working faster than humans were ever intended to, exploiting anyone who wasn't a rich white male to keep rich white men in power, creating laws and regulations to keep non-white people in their place, and so much more caused our entire country to come to a screeching halt when the Great Depression hit. It's like that moment when running on fumes for too long finally catches up to you. You inevitably tap out and realize this life isn't working like you thought it was, and something needs to change ASAP. During the Great Depression, our society hit its first major wall and caused many to realize *this isn't sustainable*.

Yet we didn't seem to learn our lesson. We paused . . . for a second. We made a few radical changes to the capitalist system we had built thus far. We realized that people needed at least *some* help from the government, so America built its first social safety net, shifted ownership of many facilities from private to public (this is important), and constituted guaranteed income for families.[26] FDR's New Deal constructed public housing projects for non-defense-work civilians to assist with the housing crisis. The Federal Housing Administration (FHA) was created to ensure white families could purchase a home at an affordable rate, later expanding assistance to those returning home from World War II.[27] It was America's first time exploring the idea of actually helping its people and introducing a modernized, lite version of that village mentality again.

However, those privileges were only afforded to a certain group of people. The elderly, minorities, and those living in poverty (who were always overwhelmingly BIPOC) were mostly left out of this new village.[28] The introduction of the FHA also meant the introduction of *redlining*, which was a strategy used to keep Black families from securing home mortgages, forcing them to uproot themselves and resettle in segregated and underfunded public housing. The assistance white families received to purchase a home, find a good job, and create an affordable life for themselves led to a false idea of meritocracy.[29]

We're led to believe that the American Dream is achieved when we follow all of those rules we talked about earlier and tick the right boxes: college, job, marriage, and house in the suburbs. The doors are supposedly wide open; it's just our responsibility to walk through them and "make it happen." Yet the majority of white families were only able to "achieve" their American Dream and begin building wealth by having access to government assistance in the 1940s, '50s, and '60s.[30] Today we look down on individuals who rely on government assistance, yet it's that same government assistance that created the white middle class, provided handouts, and labeled it the picture of success.

Once again, white supremacy kept building its house. The rotten white supremacy tree continued to grow. The walls kept going up. The branches kept extending. By the 1960s, we had a new picture of what the standard of greatness looked like: a single-family home in the suburbs, home ownership, and a successful blue-collar job.

Or, in other words, a nuclear white family.

I know this is a lot of history, and probably the longest chapter in this book, but when we look thoroughly at this history, we're finally able to see how our society was not only founded on the premise of white superiority and dominance but also has strategically maintained this premise from its founding to today.

From the laws that withheld Black citizenship to the creation of Wall Street and the New York Stock Exchange to the development of the Labor movement and the shift in how we work and live as human beings—these societal structures have always been viewed as important pieces of history to be proud of and never question. They've become so normalized that many of us have never stopped to think about how each system built off the others and constructed our modern culture, which influences every single corner of our collective society and individual lives. We'll cover a few of these systems in the next chapter.

Yes, there are many, many wonderful things Western society has built. Taking a critical look at our society doesn't negate this.

However, the glimmers of beauty in our broken world often create an illusion that everything is okay, and this is an extremely dangerous and harmful illusion we must erase. An abusive relationship often does the same thing, which is why it is so hard for victims to escape. We lie to ourselves and say, "Well, if we just fix this or do that better, everything will be okay, and the abuse won't happen again." *The abuse always happens again.* It keeps happening until you leave that relationship. We must leave our relationship with our abusive society and work together to build a new one from the ground up. We cannot let the few glimmers of gold keep us trapped in a relationship that is damaging our souls.

As you continue through this book, more history will be woven into each chapter to continue painting the picture of how white supremacy culture has stolen our self-worth. But before we conclude this chapter, we need to take a quick trip from the 1960s to today. We all know the 1950s and '60s to be an infamous period in our history when Black people stood their ground, said "Enough is enough," and fought for their civil rights. What many don't know is what followed the Civil Rights Act after it was passed and segregation was outlawed. If there is anything we can learn from history, it's that it's consistent in repeating itself. Cliché, but boy is it true.

Jim Crow, Whitelash, and Meritocracy

Within the period of modern history we've been discussing, there is a pattern of "white backlash," or *whitelash*, anytime progress is made toward a group of people that white people have oppressed to maintain their supremacy.[31] For example, after emancipation and in the midst of Reconstruction, the political, economic, and educational advancement of the newly freed Black population was quickly met with violent, white supremacist backlash in attempts to reinstate the racial social order that the South, and the United States as a whole, relied upon. When Black men received the right to vote along with their long overdue citizenship after the Fifteenth Amendment was passed, whitelash existed in the form of literacy tests, poll taxes, and deadly attacks from white supremacist mobs that kept Black people from participating in elections. Vagrancy laws were developed to force freedmen back to the plantations and back to the shackles. And the near-century-long Jim Crow era rose out of the plaguing fear of Black advancement and the desperation to maintain the nation's foundation of white supremacy.[32]

When the Civil Rights Act was passed over one hundred years after emancipation, whitelash took the form of rolling back many of the government assistance programs—which now Black people would be eligible for—that white people had benefited from to achieve middle-class status or that Americanized version of "success."[33] When Black people gained equal access to public facilities, white-controlled city councils began closing, underfunding, or privatizing public pools, community centers, parks, and so forth so that Black people wouldn't integrate them.[34] Since housing, education, and employment discrimination based on race was no longer legal, the norm became "color-blind" policies that denied considering any impact of past discrimination when trying to find a job, to advance one's education, or to purchase a home.[35] Impacts of past discrimination, including socioeconomic and education status, kept Black people at a disadvantage, but Black people were expected to be able to achieve the same levels of "success" as their white counterparts even though they were more than two hundred years "behind." The government assistance that had been available to white families and took into account their post–World War II economic struggles was not available to Black families experiencing post–Jim Crow economic disadvantages.[36]

While there were some policies created by President Lyndon B. Johnson to close the racial wealth and achievement gaps, known as the Great Society, they were short-lived due to both the war in Vietnam taking precedence and backlash from white citizens who didn't think Black citizens should receive any "handouts."[37] However, some progress was made with these policies during their short tenure. The poverty rates within the Black community began to decline, and the Black middle class began to grow.[38] But, as history has taught us, we know exactly what happens as soon as Black people begin to make progress: whitelash.

The War on Poverty, created by President Johnson to aid the Black community, was followed by the War on Drugs, created by President Nixon, to criminalize and deter the progress of the Black community.[39] At the same time, lawmakers wrote the false narrative that Johnson's policies were to blame for the record-high inflation and economic downfall of the 1970s, even though the majority of the downfall was caused by high spending from the Vietnam War.[40] As a result, Black people were painted as useless freeloaders who were just abusing the welfare system to collect government checks and remain unemployed, even though nothing could have been further from the truth.

This is yet another theme we see in history: when things are happening in the world that hurt our economy, policies that benefit the Black community, as well as other disadvantaged communities, are usually the first to be blamed for that negative economic impact even though they typically have very little to do with it. From labeling Black mothers as welfare queens, to Ronald Reagan using the campaign slogan *Get those welfare bums back to work* during his 1966 run for California governor, to spreading the false idea that the Civil Rights Act violated the liberties of white people who opposed it, to using racist scare tactics to promote a "tough on crime"

approach to control the "raging crime and drugs that were running rampant within Black neighborhoods," white leaders had exactly the rhetoric they needed to convince their white constituents
that every single policy that benefitted Black people needed to be
eradicated.[41]

No matter how false the narrative, if it comes from people in
positions of power, it will influence the minds of their constituents.
So, of course, these narratives spread like wildfire. However, since
overt racist motives were no longer legal when creating laws and
regulations, coded language was used to create policies that would
maintain and further white supremacy while disguising it as "economic freedom."[42] A push for the return to a free market economy
had been growing since FDR's New Deal era, and with the growing
frustration white people had toward post–Civil Rights Act desegre-
gation and racial-restoration policies, free market economists saw
their opportunity to finally persuade a shift in the current economic
ideology. Essentially, if legal racial discrimination was no longer
allowed, then policies that assist Black people with any type of advancement shouldn't be allowed either. No, no. Now that's "racism."
Instead, everyone should just have "economic freedom," and what
they choose to do with it is "their individual responsibility."[43] So,
even though it was quite clear that the majority of Black Americans
were centuries behind their white counterparts due to over two
hundred years of stolen labor plus nearly one hundred years of Jim
Crow—all while white people simultaneously received plenty of
government handouts to get ahead—now government assistance
and involvement in any capacity was simply out of the question.
Unless, of course, it was to instill "law and order," which was just
code for "do something with those Black people" or "make sure
America's richest individuals and corporations remain in power
. . . and remain white."[44]

Thus, the free market economy (also known as neoliberalism) as we know it today was officially born. And if you're still a bit unsure as to what that means, it's basically the economic structure we've had from Reagan's presidency to today that advocates for as little government assistance or involvement in our lives as possible.[45] Logistically, this happens by way of cutting government spending for social safety net programs (or eliminating them completely), mandating the deregulation of private industry (allowing the freedom to exploit and cheat for capital gain), facilitating the privatization and marketization of public sector institutions (programs once public and free for whites only were now private and expensive to keep them inaccessible to BIPOC and other marginalized people), and making policy decisions that ensured wealth and power remained where they "rightfully" belonged.[46] Basically, protection of our human rights of fairness, equity, and equality went out the window.[47] Why? Because we should all be able to "pull ourselves up by our bootstraps" and "earn our economic standing" even though we inhabit a society still reeling from the injustices of its founding, making this a nearly unattainable feat.

While this new way of handling the economy was motivated by the strongest desire to maintain the racial hierarchy without publicly admitting it, these economic policies would soon catch up with everyone, no matter their race, class, or gender identity. With this shift in economic policy, the standard of white success shifted too. We went from a nuclear, middle-class white family with blue-collar jobs being the picture of the "American Dream" to just the white elite (i.e., the top 1%) being the picture of success and *just the white elite* receiving most of the support from the leaders of our nation. Either way, white supremacy and whiteness remain as the gold standard. However, now this gold standard has become nearly unobtainable not just for non-white folks but for everyone.

Disclaimer: there is a lot of history I wasn't able to cover, such as specific discriminatory and racist practices against other marginalized groups. This is a brief overview with the aim of showing how the main systemic structures of our society are rooted in anti-Blackness and white supremacy. Also, this history is not to illustrate that only white people are wealthy and only BIPOC are victims of poverty but rather is simply proof of the attempt to maintain racial hierarchy and white supremacy. Of course, there are several instances of individual resistance that prove these attempts were not always successful. Nevertheless, these individual stories do not negate the system of white supremacy our society relies on.

It Wasn't an Accident

So, we've just covered hundreds of years of history in only a few pages! Let's do a quick recap, since I know that was *a lot*. From the late fifteenth and early sixteenth centuries, the development of our modern society as we know it has been built on the premise that anyone and anything that resembled Blackness in any way was inferior. As a result, whiteness became the superior standard culture, way of life, image of beauty, and everything in between. Every single movement, decision, policy, structure, ideal, theory, and norm has operated from this foundation, and it has resulted in creating a culture that each of us has unknowingly succumbed to.

The earliest colonizers believed they had a divine mission from God to build a world that submitted only to "Christian" authority and a "Christian lifestyle" that was just a European lifestyle viewed as more civilized, proper, and representative of Christian salvation. Everyone else was forced to essentially surrender their cultural practices, religions, and other standards to bow down to the way of life being created under the mantle of white supremacy.

The development of our society was based on the idea that Black and other non-white people were barbaric animals that must be contained, controlled, saved from themselves, and prevented from ever having equal access to the world that white people rightly dominate. However, it is in these racist practices that white supremacy became the enemy of the very people who created it and did everything to protect it. White people raised the bar of humanity so high that even *they* can no longer attain it.

I've talked you through this history because I want you to see the bigger picture and how that picture was created conquest by conquest, law by law. I want you to take a good look at every single rotten root of white supremacy and recognize how we got here. I want you to be able to see how both enslavement and colonization are just as vital as the Industrial Revolution, Jim Crow, and twentieth-century economic policies in the construction of our white supremacist society. Therefore, you can see that our current struggles are no accident.

It is also no accident that so many are waking up to the realities of white supremacy right now. It is no accident that we are critically looking at how it breeds capitalism, patriarchy, misogyny, sexism, ableism, and more, and how each one of those, in turn, feeds the way we evaluate ourselves and each other.

A bunch of European men gave themselves power by brutally stealing humanity and dignity from other nations, and they set out to construct a world that bowed down to them. And they were successful. This world they created taught us that it was okay to exploit others for our personal gain and that it was okay to allow others to exploit us for theirs. We learned that the only thing that matters is the wealth of our nation and those in power, instead of our livelihoods, health, and well-being.

They created a world with unattainable standards, and unless you're one of the privileged few who receive secret help to attain those standards, you will burn out trying to "make it," to no avail. The result? A crazed society that is highly addicted to stress, perfectionism, and burning the candle at both ends with a people who tie their productivity, socioeconomic status, education level, ability to maintain an unnatural and unrealistic Eurocentric standard of beauty, and unhealthy levels of self-sufficiency to their intrinsic worth as human beings. Surely this is enough to make anyone experience an immense amount of grief and self-doubt.

Our society is rife with staggering inequalities that have only gotten worse with time. We see racial wealth and achievement gaps that seem to just grow wider instead of narrower, an economy that feels nearly impossible to live comfortably in, mental health crises and suicide seeing their highest rates ever in history, and physical health challenges that continue to skyrocket. We see BIPOC communities continue to be marginalized, along with the LGBTQIA+ and disabled communities, as well as many other societal and economic disparities.

And that is the reason for this book: a society of humans, like you and me, have been struggling with feeling worthy our entire lives and *never quite understanding why*. But now we know why. It wasn't us this entire time. It was the system. The society. The culture, passed down from generation to generation from the very beginning of the construction of racist ideas. And now we are the generation with the power to change the narrative for ourselves and shape the narrative for generations to come. We are the ones who get to say, "Enough is enough. We refuse to spend our entire lives proving ourselves when we were already worthy from the moment we were born."

From this moment forward, we are free.

Journal Prompts

1. How has the historical development of white supremacy impacted the way I view myself as an individual? How has it affected my self-worth?

2. What historical developments stand out the most to me? What historical developments and ideologies did I use to believe as truth that I now realize are fallacies?

Part 2

Reclaiming
Our Worth

4

Where We First Learned to Be White

I am so stupid, I thought to myself as I listened to the whirlwind of intelligent discourse between my classmates in my advanced placement European history class.

It didn't matter how much of the chapter I had read the night before class to prepare, or how many lunch periods I spent with my teacher going over concept after concept—I just could not keep up. Our desks were set in a circle so we could all be a part of the roundtable discussion. Every sixth period, I would begrudgingly walk into the classroom, set my materials on my desk, and succumb to the feelings of inferiority and defeat as I watched my classmates hold collegiate-level conversations that made me feel increasingly insignificant with each passing minute.

In my junior year of high school, European history was one of the advanced placement classes I forced myself to take to look more qualified for college on my high school transcript. The first thing my mother had asked the school principal when I entered my freshman year was, "What are the requirements for receiving an honors diploma?" "You must take at least two advanced courses every year," she replied. My mom faced me and said, "Do you hear that? Two advanced courses each year."

I nodded my head in agreement. It had been drilled into my head that taking those classes was nonnegotiable. It was one of those things on my "Work twice as hard because you are Black" checklist. It was my training for the world I was getting ready to enter. A world that would want nothing to do with me as a Black woman unless I had something to show for myself. It didn't matter if the advanced courses were, in fact, too advanced for me. It didn't matter if I learned at a different pace or required a different learning style than my peers. The title "advanced" was more important than what I was learning; my grade point average and honors status took precedence over everything else until my spot at a prestigious university was secured.

I often spent those roundtable discussions by finding a focal point to stare at on the wall of the classroom, drowning out the intimidating discussion with my self-deprecating thoughts, and hoping the teacher wouldn't notice my lack of contribution. I never had any idea what they were talking about. I could barely keep up with what a monarchy was versus a parliament, and whether we were talking about Queen Elizabeth I or II. My grade in that class the first trimester reflected my confusion: a solid C−, which was the worst grade I'd ever received. That C− was not indicative of laziness or neglecting to complete my assignments. I made every note card, highlighted every page of my textbook, took copious notes during lectures, and spent the entire following trimester having additional study sessions during lunch with my teacher instead of eating with my (very few) friends. That was the trimester I somehow managed a B–, and I'm pretty sure it's because my teacher bumped my grade out of pity, because my comprehension of the material did not improve.

I was always the only Black kid in my advanced courses. We only had a handful of BIPOC students in my school, and that's, regretfully, exactly why I chose to attend. I thought that a white high school would grant me a better education than a high school in the city with a larger population of non-white students. So, when it came time to enroll in high school and my mom asked me if I wanted to try attending a school in the district she worked for in the city, I immediately said, "No way."

Living in the suburbs and attending predominantly white schools with only white teachers and a whitewashed approach to education was all I knew. Because those demographics matched society's picture of success, I believed it was a better option than attending a school in a community that was representative of my lived experience as a Black person.

I did everything I could to try to be exactly like my white peers. I spoke like them, dressed like them, listened to their music, read their books, and watched their TV shows. I read their beauty magazines and took their advice on how to shrink my stomach, apply eyeliner, and straighten my hair. Because I believed that every characteristic that came from white people represented intelligence, beauty, and success, I did everything in my power to assimilate into their world. Every teacher I had from kindergarten to twelfth grade was a white person. And in every classroom, I was almost always the only one, or one of two, Black students in the class.

My world was divided. In my Black world, I was fortunate to see greatness, intelligence, beauty, and success when I looked at my adoptive parents and other members of my family. Both my mother and father held college degrees, with my father having received a PhD in chemistry. My godmother and godfather were both elementary school principals, and my mother was a director of a diversity program for a local school district. My father was a professor at a Big 10 university and did extensive work with the National Science Foundation. The social organizations they were members of consisted of numerous Black professionals who held top positions within their career fields. I was regularly surrounded by Black excellence. Expectations were high, and I had big shoes to fill. However, whenever I looked at my role models, I saw them often being the lone, or one of few, Black professionals in their fields, and I internalized how their mannerisms changed when they were in those settings. Every single word bounced off their tongues with precise articulation. Every outfit they wore was carefully picked out, pressed, and ready to impress. Never a single hair was out of place, always transformed from kinky to straight with a relaxer and a hot comb. With the obvious exception of actually changing their skin color, they looked and sounded just like the white teachers and leaders that were a part of my daily life, as well as all of the white leaders and influential figures I saw in the media. As Black professionals, it seemed as though they were the anomaly, and that they had to put on a presentation of whiteness to be in those positions.

———

The bell rang, and I snapped out of my stupor. Everyone in my class was gathering their belongings, and once again I felt like the biggest failure. I pulled out my Product(Red) iPod, plugged in the headphones, blasted the most emo song I could find, and trudged through the sea of happy-go-lucky white kids to my next class. Ding! The bell rang again. iPod, emo song, repeat. Each class reminded me just how much I felt like I didn't belong and would never measure up to the white kids or my brilliant parents and their high expectations. I felt so isolated even though I was constantly surrounded by people.

Ding! Ding! Ding!

On the outside, I seemed like a picture-perfect Black girl who was doing all the right things that would lead me to be a picture-perfect successful Black woman. Take honors courses. Check. Curate an extensive extracurricular activity schedule. Check. Maintain a part-time job. Check. Stay out of trouble. Check. Maintain a minimum 3.5 grade point average. Che . . . nope. I could only manage a 3.4, and while that difference seems so minuscule now, I was reminded every single day of my shortcoming. Above all else, this was the top requirement from my parents, and this was the requirement I failed. Sure, it was nice that I was a member of the band and per-formed in the school play, but nothing was as important as that grade point average. But no matter how hard I tried, I just couldn't pull off that 3.5.

School was incredibly hard for me, but my frustrations were often met with pushback, so I swallowed my anxieties and continued to drive myself as I was told to do. If I wasn't making the grades, it was because *I* wasn't working hard enough. If I wasn't understanding the material, it was because *I* wasn't doing everything I could to make sure I got it. I just had to be proactive, ask every teacher for extra help, do the extra credit, take more notes, study longer, retake all of my tests, and keep pushing myself until my GPA reflected my efforts. That was the only answer. This was my fault, and it was *my responsi-bility* to fix it. Not anyone else. That was just how the world worked. (This is individualism at its finest—society-bred internalized guilt, shame, and failure for having the very human need for *help*.)

I wish I could go back in time and give sixteen-year-old Caroline the biggest hug. Gosh, she so desperately needed a hug. She felt so alone, so unworthy, and was so often near the brink of a breakdown without anyone ever realizing it. I would have held her and said, "Stop. This is not your fault. You have worked so hard. You are being forced to demonstrate your learning in a way that only benefits some students and sets most students up for failure in some capacity. You're being forced to take in too much information at one time, and it's too much for your body and mind to go through at once. And that's okay. It doesn't make you a failure. It makes you human. You're burned out, you need a break, and you need to stop allowing anyone to put pressure on you. You are doing such a good job."

We all need to take a moment and tell our sixteen-year-old selves what they ache to hear. Give yourself permission to do that right now.

Inhale: *It wasn't my fault.* Exhale: *I am worthy.*

Whiteness Is Standard

The school system is one of the first places that we learn we must measure up to a specific standard, and if we don't, we aren't good enough. At the tender age of five, most of us officially start school and immediately enter into the system of white supremacy that rules our society. This system tells us that there is only *one right way* to become a fully functional adult, and that "right" way has been defined by a wealth-chasing capitalist society that no longer honors the beautiful complexities and natural rhythms of our unique beings.

This society, which once freely declared, "Kill the Indian, save the man," while forcing Indigenous children into residential schools and stripping them of all dignity and humanity.[1] This society, which once denied Black people the chance to learn how to read and write in order to maintain our ignorance and brainwash us into obedience. This society, which committed atrocities against so many people yet twisted the truth and taught future generations that those atrocities were warranted out of a divine, manifested destiny from God, and without these defensible acts of violence, we wouldn't have the "land of the free" we are so fortunate to live in today.

Oh, and the same society has placed legal bans on teaching the truth to today's youth to make sure this fallacy continues to be sold as truth when today's youth become tomorrow's leaders. But I digress.

Each of these destructive, calamitous ideas continues to serve as the cornerstone for what we learn in school. We learn that any culture, lifestyle, religion, ethnicity, or other identity that doesn't align with *white* and *Christian* is somehow wrong, abnormal, and inferior. We learn that our native tongues must give way to standard English and that any accent or cultural dialect is unacceptable in our whitewashed world. We learn that our cultural foods are "unhealthy" and must give way to only foods that American diet culture and nutrition textbooks deem as healthy, leading us to feel shame about the ethnic foods that grace our dinner tables at home. We learn that the natural curvature of our hips and thighs is considered ugly and unhealthy in comparison to the slender, thin, white bodies that are put on a pedestal in both fashion magazines and our health textbooks.

We learn that our natural instincts to honor our body's rhythms are somehow lazy and unproductive, and we internalize guilt and shame should we want or need to rest. We learn that the only way to make it in this world is to hustle—race to the top and don't look back at who you knocked over to get there. We learn that the value of our humanity is solely based on so-called measurable markers of success and what that "success" will allow us to produce for a society that does so little for us in return.

Whenever I think back to my memories of kindergarten, a dark cloud looms in my spirit. My five-year-old self couldn't articulate it, but I knew exactly where my place was in that class. My milk chocolate skin and big, frizzy hair stuck out like a sore thumb amongst my blond-haired, blue-eyed, fair-skinned peers. Friends didn't come easy, except for the one other Black girl in the other kindergarten class down the hall. You all remember her from the prelude.

The pressure to perform was immediate. One moment, play and innocence were the most important things in my little brain, and the next, I was stressed out about my test scores and what consequences I would receive if they weren't good enough. My first memories of feeling like I was drowning in a world that wasn't built for me were in *kindergarten.* No five-year-old should ever have to experience such immense pressure, but this is the norm in our classrooms. This pressure is a value that is upheld in the highest regard, because that "pressure" is meant to ensure children are equipped to endure the world and contribute to the marketplace when it's finally their turn.

From day one, buzz phrases like "college readiness" and questions about what kids want to be when they grow up are commonplace. Immediately, children are conditioned to think about their identity in terms of a vocation rather than their unique attributes that demonstrate just how fearfully and wonderfully made they are. The capitalist agenda promptly begins, but it's disguised as the American Dream: "Work hard, get good grades, go to college, get a job, and make something of yourself. That is the key to success. That is the key to happiness. That is the key to freedom."

Yet that promised freedom is nothing short of a mirage. An illusion that draws you in, hypnotizing you into the system. Dazed, you unknowingly walk onto the white supremacy conveyor belt with no end in sight.

The goal: mold yourself into an object whose sole purpose and worth are based on your ability to produce and consume in the global marketplace.

The real result: dehumanization.

School is the first place we are taught that we must conform ourselves to society's ideal version of a human being: one who performs perfectly, submits to authority without question (even in instances of harm), remains objective and logical, and shames or shuts down emotion while focusing on a quantitative version of success over a qualitative one. School is the place we are conditioned into white supremacy culture, adopting its characteristics as norms while remaining completely unaware of the harm it causes.

At the same time, school is also often the only safe haven children know. School is where we meet that first adult, outside of our parents, who is somehow able to see deep into our souls and care for us in the way we longed to be cared for but never dared to ask for. Some of us were lucky enough to be able to call both school and home a safe haven, but for so many, that safe haven was only ever school.

School is where thirty million US children get their guaranteed hot meal every day.[2] It is where many kids get their only hug or attention from an adult and are finally able to feel seen as a person. It is where children who have been forced to grow up too soon get to play, laugh, and run before they come home to take on responsibilities that were only ever meant for adults.

Our school system is filled with the most incredible teachers who show up to work every day while enduring abuse from the school system and their communities and receiving non-livable pay. And they do so because they believe in every single child who enters their classroom and will bend over backward to make sure that child sees a future for themselves.

I don't believe our teachers have any desire to indoctrinate their students into white supremacy culture. It's just that, like all of us, they are at the mercy of a system none of us had any hand in developing. Just like they have to uphold their students to standards they didn't create, they are also held to standards that strategically make sure the education they are providing falls in line with the white supremacy agenda. And, because white supremacy culture is the norm for all of us, we inadvertently perpetuate it every day, unknowingly causing harm to ourselves and those around us.

We are not all affected by white supremacy in the same way—white supremacy will always cause more harm to Black, Indigenous, People of Color than to its white constituents whom the system was originally built to honor and protect. We can see that firsthand in our public school system with the blatant discrepancies between schools that serve predominantly Black or non-white populations versus schools that serve predominantly white populations. (Read: the school to prison pipeline, underfunded schools, and achievement gaps, but I don't have time to go off on that tangent right now.)

In curating a system that puts the characteristics of white, upper- and middle-class people at the center while telling everyone else that this is the standard, *everyone* is harmed. If you happen to be part of the demographic that is labeled the picture of perfection, you face the pressure to reach for and maintain that standard and never, ever break. If you're part of the demographic that is labeled as the opposite of the picture of perfection, you spend your entire life fighting the uphill battle of trying to become that picture, all while thinking that until you do so, you are not good enough. Or you succumb to the narrative that's been written for you. Either way, nobody wins.

I recently shared my story about how I secretly struggled in school with a friend, and they were in total shock. And a bit of denial. "But you handled everything so well! You were so popular! You were one of the most visible students in your high school! You had a superb experience!"

See, in the Black community, admitting difficulty is often perceived as ungratefulness. And that makes sense. The plight of the Black community has always been the backbone of our story. Our legacy doesn't get to stand independent from our freedom song. Our triumphs only exist because of the abuses we have endured—spending our existence proving ourselves worthy to the white society that was built to keep us in chains. Each generation has fought like hell, praying that their fight would allow the next generation to taste a fraction more of the freedom that white men get to drink in abundance. The audacity of a young person grumbling without ever walking a mile in the previous generation's shoes feels like a slap in the face. How could I whine about my experience as a student when I was lucky enough to go to one of the best schools in my state, to never have to withstand the horrors of the Jim Crow South, and to have access to a public education my ancestors would have never been able to dream of? How dare I?

Toxicity loves to disguise itself as progress. And progress is the language of white supremacy culture. It is always measured as "bigger" or "more." Always quantitatively, never qualitatively. Our culture of white supremacy trains us to suppress the emotional toll of the grueling nature of our society with gratitude for all of the "progress" we have made. This allows us to conveniently forget that we are on the white supremacy conveyor belt, blindly submitting to white supremacy's authority. If anything, it gets us to buy into the conveyor belt. We agree with it, because its buttery language confuses us into believing that it is the best thing that has ever happened to us—while it is simultaneously crushing our souls.

The same exact thing happened on the plantations. As the cotton industry grew, plantation owners turned their plantations into complex hierarchical factory systems, incentivizing enslaved people who consistently met their picking quota with leadership positions such as head drivers and specialists. Enslaved workers in those "higher" positions were tasked with supervising other enslaved workers, which bred the idea of superiority while pitting workers against each other.[3] But they were all still *enslaved*. Read that again. They were still enslaved—in chains, lashes on their backs, bonded to the system, believing that their taste of success somehow granted them closer proximity to freedom.

In the twenty-first century, each one of us still lives in bondage to the system of white supremacy, as we learned in the last chapter. While it has presented itself differently throughout history, and societal advancements have allowed it to disguise itself nearly to the point of undetectability, the overarching system has never changed. It's just evolved. The evolved system, and the detriment it has caused, is why I lament my difficulties. I may not have experienced segregated, run-down school buildings. I may not have been spat on and called the N-word to my face. But I still attended a school built within a system created to instill the false ideals of white supremacy culture into every child that walked through its doors. Especially BIPOC children. And I am not the only one.

The Fear of Educated Black People and the Creation of Educational "Standards"

The biggest threat to white supremacy is not Black existence. It's Black advancement. Black progress. Black education. Black existence is welcomed when Black people are kept where white supremacy claims we belong: providing free labor at the expense of our humanity to preserve white progress and power. As long as we have those proverbial shackles around our feet, we are palatable in the eyes of white supremacy.

During the untold historical truth of the Reconstruction era, Black advancement was robust. Even with many of the Southern state leaders loudly opposing the abolition of enslavement, the Fourteenth and Fifteenth Amendments established Black citizenship and suffrage, and Black men were granted the right to vote and hold political office at every possible level. Education, once denied to every member of the Black race, began to flourish.

The founding of the public school system was one of the main initiatives from the Reconstruction era that was the most imperative to the Black community.[4] Black families were rightfully insistent their children attend school after over two hundred years of being denied the right to an education, and they played a major role in the establishment of the public school system. Free, universal education allowed for both Black and non-wealthy white families to achieve considerable literacy advancements, which had previously been privatized and reserved for wealthy white families. However, as we can remember from the whitelash section of the previous chapter, it wasn't long before the Jim Crow South emerged, forcing Black children to attend separate, unequal, and underfunded public schools.

The fear of Black advancement has controlled every corner of our public school system since the violent overthrow of Reconstruction policies. When we think of racism in our schools, we usually think solely of segregation and the 1954 *Brown v. Board of Education* Supreme Court case that ruled segregation in public schools unconstitutional.[5] That's about the extent of what we learn in our social studies classes, and that is no accident. The mission of fulfilling the false American narrative of meritocracy and unfailing freedom ensures that the truth about our racist foundation and white supremacist agenda is never revealed, leaving us to learn bite-sized, sugar-coated, and mostly untruthful accounts of our history in school. We learn that *Brown v. Board of Education* ended segregation in public schools and that upon integration, Black and white kids essentially held hands and skipped down the hallways together singing "Kumbaya."

The truth is that the Supreme Court ruling spurred on even more racism out of desperation for white control. The fear of Black progress prevailed once again. White families did not want their precious, "pure" white schools to be stained with the presence of Black children, nor did they want Black children to have access to the higher quality of public education their children were receiving, so they began to form private schools to get around the legal demands to integrate public schools.[6]

In some instances, entire school districts closed down in efforts to keep Black students from walking through their doors. And this is the nice, flowery way to explain all of this, but let's be real—countless Black children were inhumanly attacked for daring to set foot in a white school when integration was mandated.[7] White rage made itself known and resorted to violence like it always does. And it succeeded like it always does. Just look at our public school system right now, and you will see the clear evidence of segregated and unequal schools between white neighborhoods and Black neighborhoods, and an ever-growing racial achievement gap to go right along with it.[8] This is not a coincidence.

The achievement gap between white children and their BIPOC peers was physically concocted to preserve and uphold white supremacy. Literally. The media, lawmakers, and the Department of Education would love for us to believe that this gap exists because Black families make poor choices and just can't seem to prioritize education like their white counterparts do. No, no.

Before integration was even a thing, eugenicists and racist, xenophobic psychologists were busy creating standardized testing for the sole purpose of proving the superiority of white people and preserving social order.[9] With the rise in immigration and the growing demands for equal rights by the Black community, fear of the changing racial and class hierarchy caused eugenicists to incite political propaganda that successfully influenced white families to believe that an increase in immigration and integration would lead to a steady decline of the public school system.

Carl Brigham, a prominent psychologist and eugenicist who developed aptitude tests used in World War I, believed that testing would prove the superiority of the Nordic race and the inferiority of the Black race. At the request of the College Board, he created the Standardized Aptitude Test (SAT) to not only prove his theory but to reinforce the racial hierarchy and keep Black people from advancing their education.[10] These tests, of course, were created from a Eurocentric lens with Eurocentric bias, and they did exactly what they were designed to do: uphold the idea that whiteness was the gold standard of intelligence. By the 1930s, multiple-choice tests were firmly entrenched in American schools and remain today as one of the primary ways students are expected to prove their intellect, regardless of countless data that show such tests are ineffective as well as racially, ethnically, and culturally biased.[11]

Standards have become the everyday economy of our public schools. While learning standards differ slightly from state to state, the overarching theme is abundantly clear: children learn from a Eurocentric lens in every subject so that their whiteness conditioning is automatic, while rarely considering other cultural viewpoints, contributions, and academic frameworks that are just as profound and important to our world.[12]

The Eurocentric lens not only frames what we are taught in the core curriculum but *how* we are taught and how we are expected to demonstrate meeting and exceeding the standards set for us. This is done with the utmost intent within every corner of our education system. Curriculum-wise, learning only Western notions of literacy, math, science, and social studies, along with untruthful narratives about Western dominance, infuse into our educational foundations anti-Blackness that is nearly impossible to undo. With this foundation, children are primed to continue the false narrative of superiority that America, and the rest of the Western world, has been writing since the fifteenth century.

The moment you enter your first classroom, your value as a human being is replaced with your value being contingent upon your ability to adhere to the standards set before you. You are now a product, and your performance measurements are your test scores and grade point averages. You are taught by devoted educators who show up every day in an attempt to fight the system—they know what it's doing to you, and they wish they could change it, but they can't. They don't make the decisions. They are expected to somehow make sure their students with diverse needs and backgrounds all meet these standards at a pace many adults with professional degrees wouldn't be able to handle.

When students struggle to meet those standards, the demands increase, as if somehow increasing demands and pushing children harder will magically make students "rise to the occasion," because clearly, their struggles are their fault in the first place. Please sense my sarcasm here. Our educational pedagogy is filled with demands for more rigor and higher standards as the fear of not being able to compete with the rest of the world and uphold our capitalist powerhouse directly falls on children who just want to be kids. The result? Children are dehumanized, desensitized, and taught that unless they fit perfectly into the very narrow, standardized box of what is deemed successful by society, there is something wrong with them.

Let me rephrase that: *we* were dehumanized, desensitized, and taught that unless we fit perfectly into the very narrow, standardized box of what is deemed successful by society, there is something wrong with *us*.

Hear me when I say this: there is absolutely nothing wrong with you. You were never meant to fit into a box.

No one is.

There is no standard for being human. There is no standard measure of culture, there is no standard measure of learning, there is no standard measure of intelligence, and there is no standard measure of achievement. Everything you have been told you have to measure up to was created by a society with a very specific agenda, and that agenda only cares about what your level of production can do for their bottom line, regardless of what it does to your humanity.

It's not you, it's them.

The Grave Cost of Striving for Whiteness

"You only have a 3.4 GPA and you only earned a 24 on your ACT? That's not good enough. We don't give scholarships to students like you here."

My heart dropped to my stomach, but I continued to look him directly in the eyes, never showing my despair, while he continued to berate me. I drowned out the rest of his words. Something about how they only accepted the best of the best, that all of the students of color on scholarship held a 3.8 GPA or higher, and that I should have worked harder if I wanted a scholarship to his prestigious university.

I was on a college tour at a prominent, predominantly white university I had already been accepted into. Every spring, this university held a tradition of hosting a weekend for all the students of color who had been accepted into the university for the following year. As my college acceptance letters were slowly rolling in, I was weighing the options of where to attend, and one of the major factors of consideration was whether or not I would receive scholarship money from the school. I was graduating high school during the Great Recession, and somehow the government thought that my single working mother had the means to fork over $40,000 annually for my education. That was well over half of her income, but sure, government, that makes sense. (Insert eye-roll emoji.) I had already applied for dozens of outside scholarships and received a few of them, but none were enough to mitigate the hefty cost of tuition at any of the colleges to which I'd been accepted.

When I was invited to this exclusive weekend by this particular university, my mom and I thought it would be a great opportunity to make some connections and see what I could do to get a scholarship. We were feeling optimistic. Receiving an invitation to this special all-expenses-paid visit, which included mentorship from current students of color and attendance at an invite-only luncheon to speak with various deans and professors, made it seem as though this university thought I was a highly qualified candidate and wanted me to pick them. Not to mention I thought I deserved a scholarship. At least a partial one.

I knew that my GPA and ACT scores fell just a tad short of their scholarship requirements, but I also knew myself and just how much I brought to the table. The fact that I even sustained a 3.4 GPA while maintaining active involvement in as many extracurriculars as I did, I thought, wasn't half bad. I was one of the leading competitors on the speech team, was one of the leading student anchors on our student news program, played many lead roles in our school plays, played varsity tennis, was a mentor to freshman students, volunteered in the special education classroom after school and at a women's shelter on the weekends, was involved in my church, maintained a part-time job at Dairy Queen, and had even been selected to be a teen reporter with our local news station's weekend teen segment. I was hopeful that my talents, passions, skills, and servant heart would be more than enough for this university to see me and say, "We'd be honored to pay for your education. You're worth it."

Instead, they took one look at my scores and said, "You don't meet the standard. Next!" and shut me down before I could blink twice.

I will never forget that feeling. I had spent years hating myself, fully embodying the belief that I was not good enough and wearing long-sleeved shirts even in the summertime to cover up the scars of self-punishment on my wrists, successfully fooling everyone who crossed my path with a fake smile, boundless energy, and over-achieving spirit. I thought that if I could just push myself as hard as possible, I would finally prove to myself and everyone around me that I was worth something. I thought that my senior year of high school would be the year I would be able to lay out my list of accomplishments, college scholarships included, and say, "Did I finally make everyone proud? Am I finally good enough? Am I finally worthy?"

The standards of whiteness are nearly impossible to assimilate. And, by the wildly unlikely chance we are able to achieve these standards, we do so at a grave cost to ourselves. We physically, mentally, emotionally, and spiritually deteriorate when we run at the pace our culture demands of us.

I've told one side of this school story. The side of the perfectionist overachiever. That is how I coped with the never-ending pressure to perform and achieve perfection from the first day of kindergarten. That is how I internalized the white supremacy conditioning I was

101

receiving and responded to it. Obviously, this isn't everyone's story. This may not be your story.

Maybe you were the student who aced every test, maintained that 4.0 GPA, received an abundance of college scholarships, and was the most popular kid in class. You loved school, you loved to learn, and you loved the thrill of overachieving. Yet underneath that 4.0 was a physical body desperate for rest and care, but you never heeded your body's cries. Now, you're dealing with long-term health complications from a body that was withering away as you refused it the care it needed.

Or maybe receiving a C in a class was a feat for you, and failing grades were your norm because keeping up with the coursework was beyond your capabilities. Maybe you sat in the back of each class, using humor and causing distractions to avoid facing the daunting assignments you struggled to read. Now, as an adult, you've finally put the pieces of the puzzle together: learning disability, ADHD, or another neurodivergence. It makes so much sense now, but you spent your entire childhood wondering why you were the one who was "different," feeling like a failure when, in reality, it was the system that failed you.

And maybe you were lucky if you even made it to school every day. School was your safe haven. You knew you would be fed, you had friends you could count on, and for a few hours every day you could escape the turmoil you experienced at home. But, because of such turmoil, school was the least of your priorities. You gave it your all, but you also wondered when this world you were preparing for was going to give its all to you. You experienced firsthand the suffering of being part of the corner of society whose labor isn't honored with livable wages and whose existence seems to be ignored but also exploited for the gain of the already wealthy, privileged, and powerful.

Maybe you see a bit of yourself in each scenario. Maybe I haven't covered anything close to your story, and you're still struggling to feel seen right now. If that's the case, I deeply apologize. I recognize that I am writing about the impacts of white supremacy culture in our society from my narrow perspective, and I know that hearing others' stories can be both helpful and triggering. I always want to acknowledge that I know I won't be able to cover every angle perfectly. I give myself grace for that while also acknowledging that it may cause you to feel even more unseen. Please know that even if I didn't talk about your perspective directly, I do see you. I see that you are reading this book right now because you are determined to figure out the source of your unworthiness battle. I see that you have been hurting. I see that you have most likely spent your life wondering when you will ever love yourself and feel fully worthy right where you are without having to prove yourself to anyone.

The Enemy Is Always White Supremacy

I want you to understand that school itself is not the enemy here. Just like your parents are not the enemy, nor is every other institution we talk about in this book. The enemy is white supremacy. The enemy has always been white supremacy. White supremacy lords over our society, and every single institution within our society has no choice but to succumb to it. We shall have no other gods before our God, yet so-called followers of Jesus created a god in white supremacy and built an entire society that has been intrinsically designed to worship that god. Unless we actively resist doing so, we are worshiping the god of white supremacy. Even those of us with the best of intentions, individuals and institutions alike.

The institution of public school has the best of intentions. Every single child on this earth has the right to a free, quality education, and our teachers show up every day to do their best to give them just that. I am in no way denying the need for everyone to have the best education afforded to them, without condition, and to take that education seriously so they can develop a love for learning and a zeal for pushing themselves toward their personal best every day. I firmly believe that education is one of the main keys we all must possess to unlock our liberation. I am not anti-diligence, anti-accountability, or even anti-pressure, as long as it's healthy. And I am certainly not anti-knowledge. Not to be cliché, but knowledge is power.

The fundamental concept behind the creation of an entire system that allows children to learn everything from basic reading to the most advanced scientific concepts is golden and necessary. We must never take our access to this for granted. However, this brilliant system was built within a society that had already declared white supremacy to be its god and had no choice but to surrender to its lordship. And that surrender designed an institution that, in spite of its best qualities, serves its god and therefore also serves its god's evil desires.

———

I want you to go look in the mirror. Right now. Take this book with you.

Are you there? Good.

I want you to think about everything your school experience made you feel about yourself as a child and then say those lies out loud.

Inhale, say each lie out loud, and then say to it, "You are a lie. You do not serve me. I release you."

Now, exhale.

Every single negative thing you have ever thought about yourself as a result of your school experience, whether that be *You're worthless, You're not smart enough, You're never going to make it, You're only valuable when you are achieving something*, or anything I may have missed that pertains to your personal experience is a lie. Let it go. Your value does not lie in what you produce, your ability to meet a standard, or how many degrees you hold.

And even though we live in a society that tells us these lies every day, we have the freedom to release ourselves from carrying a burden that is not ours to carry.

On the other hand, I want you to remember that *binary thinking* is another characteristic of white supremacy culture, and it causes us to think that only one thing can be true. I've spent a lot of time pointing out the toxicity that lies in our public school system (and schools that aren't public) due to its inability as an institution to separate itself from white supremacy. However, that doesn't mean we just ignore the goodness that does come from school and our own positive experiences. I mentioned before that, for many children, school is the only safe space they know. Many of us had that one teacher who changed our lives because they saw us as humans, poured into us as if we were their own, and exposed the greatness that was inside of us that we would have otherwise never discovered. Maybe you met your best friend in first grade and she was your maid of honor at your wedding.

Two things can be true. We can acknowledge the joy something brought us while also lamenting the damage it simultaneously did to us and demand change so that damage doesn't continue. That doesn't mean we're ungrateful for having access to or experiencing something that someone else may wish they could have experienced. If something causes us harm, it causes us harm, and it's our right to acknowledge that, point out the fallacies, work toward healing, and advocate for change.

We must acknowledge the fact that our schools do indeed perpetuate white supremacy, were designed to train us toward participation in white supremacy, and, as a result, harm us all to some degree as we undergo this conditioning. We must acknowledge that this is not a school-based problem or a teacher-specific problem but a systemic problem that just demonstrates the system working exactly as it was designed to. And, as tempting as it is right now to take drastic action like refusing to send your children to public schools or marching down to the Department of Education and demanding change, remember that you are here to heal yourself first. You are here to heal from the lies you have believed about your worth so that you can live each day from here on out as the free human God created you to be.

So, right now, focus on that. Do the mirror exercise every day until you fully release those lies you've held on to for so long. Remember that healing is not overnight, so it's natural to still struggle with these beliefs even after you've practiced releasing them. That's okay. Keep going. It's all part of the process. You deserve this healing. Later on in the book, we will talk about ways to advocate for change, but your healing comes first.

Journal Prompts

1. Write down every lie your school experience made you believe about yourself. Once you have written the lies down, repeat the following in the mirror:

   a. Say each lie out loud.

   b. Then say, "You are a lie. You do not serve me. I release you."

   c. Inhale and exhale.

2. Reflect on the ideologies and cultural norms your school experience taught you and how those norms are rooted in

white supremacy. Now that you know the truth, how can you begin healing from these lies you've believed for so long? How can you begin unlearning these norms?

3. If you could hop in a time machine and advocate for your younger self in school by making policy, curriculum, or best-practice changes, what changes would you make and why? How do you think you could begin advocating for those changes for future generations as you learn more about the destruction of white supremacy and the importance of its demolition?

5

U.G.L.Y.

"I think I just won't eat all day," I whispered. "I want to make sure my stomach stays flat, and it will be easier to suck it in if I don't eat anything."

I was tucked under the covers in my bed, on the phone with my best friend. It was the night before our huge seventh-grade end-of-the-year field trip to the amusement park. This field trip was not like any other field trip. It symbolized the seventh-grade class becoming the new eighth-grade class—the highest status of "cool" one could reach in middle school. We were beginning to look like eighth graders too, our bodies more developed than they had been at the beginning of the school year.

With no dress code restrictions, this was everyone's opportunity to show off their new bodily enhancements by wearing as little clothing as possible. Girls were developing breasts and waistlines that they couldn't wait to show off by wearing a tiny bikini top, short shorts, and no T-shirt to cover up. The boys, sporting the latest muscle shirts from Abercrombie & Fitch, picked their favorite "hot girl's" hand to slip in theirs as they walked around the park—her body a match for his growing biceps and single strand of chest hair.

And then there was me. Flat chest, big belly, and no boys in muscle shirts giving me an ounce of attention. I didn't understand what was wrong with me. I seemed to be the only one with this . . . problem. I already felt less than ideal when it came to my looks since I was the only Black girl in a sea of blond-haired, blue-eyed teenage beauty. I was already more than aware of how my darker skin and bushy, curly hair were not what was considered "hot" by the white boys at my school. But why did I have to be Black, ugly, *and* have a big stomach? Why couldn't I at least look good in a crop top and low-rise jeans? Even all the Black girls I knew from my "other world" had flat stomachs, regardless of their signature Black girl curvy hips and thighs, so I knew my larger stomach had nothing to do with being Black. This was a me-problem. For whatever reason, I felt like I was cursed with a disgusting body and protruding stomach that made me look like I was six months pregnant in middle school.

I was desperate for that flat stomach. Desperate to look at least a fraction as cute as the popular girls. So, I came up with a plan for the field trip: eat a light dinner the night before, skip all of my meals the day of, and drink small sips of water to get by. Emphasis on the *small* sips—too much water also led to my stomach inflating, and I wasn't willing to take any risks. I pulled my brand-new bikini top over my tiny, uneven breasts and pulled my white capri pants over my it's-obvious-I'm-a-Black-girl thighs and butt. I looked in the mirror and took a big, deep breath, held it, and marveled at how flat my stomach could appear by just holding my breath. I practiced a few more times, threw on a T-shirt to wear until I got to the park, and headed to the bus stop.

My stomach was in knots. I had never revealed so much of my body to anyone besides my bathroom mirror. Would I be able to keep it held in all day? Would the popular girls catch on and notice that I was sucking my stomach in? What would I do when I got hungry? I didn't have the answers, but it didn't matter. Nothing was as important that day as feeling as pretty and as skinny as possible.

I've been at war with my body for as long as I can remember. I was about ten years old when a family member first pinched my armpit fat and told me to start sucking my belly in. "We can never be fat," she told me sternly.

I looked down at the beginning developments of my body. I had been completely oblivious to my physical "shortcomings" until then. From that moment forward, all my energy went to my stomach. Sucking in my stomach, grabbing my stomach any time I passed a mirror, skipping meals to see if my stomach would appear smaller, wearing baggy shirts to hide my stomach, looking at every woman and girl I encountered to see if their stomach looked like mine . . . it never did. I'll never forget how elated I felt when I caught a glimpse of my stomach in the mirror after recovering from a terrible bout of the stomach flu. Seeing the difference a few skipped meals and a "cleansing" of the body—so to speak—could make marked the beginning of disordered eating habits for years to come. I was desperate to achieve that post–stomach flu result again, but no matter how many cans of SlimFast I drank and how many hours of tennis I played, my belly just wouldn't deflate. (Yes, you read that right. SlimFast. As a teenager.)

Everywhere I turned, the message that my non-flat stomach was unacceptable was loud. Every magazine at the checkout counter screamed, "LOSE BELLY FAT NOW! HERE'S HOW!" Every celebrity I idolized on television had a flat stomach and even tinier waist, and they were on the cover of every magazine sharing their thousand crunches and thousand-calories-a-day regimens to achieve their itty-bitty figures. Popular shows like *The Biggest Loser* and *America's Next Top Model* rose to fame by publicly shaming women on television about the size of their bodies, calling any woman above a size 2 fat. From commercials for Weight Watchers and Jenny Craig, to shirtless Abercrombie & Fitch models, to popular low-cal snacks, to seeing Disney stars like Hilary Duff and Raven-Symoné being constantly fat-shamed for having average-sized bodies, fatphobia was everywhere.

Before I go any further, let me acknowledge that I am sharing my story and writing this chapter from a place of privilege. Even though I have struggled with carrying a bigger belly, I have always carried that bigger belly in an average-sized body, and I know that hearing stories of body image struggles from someone who presents as having an "acceptable" or "average" body size in our fatphobic society can be extremely triggering. No matter how much I've struggled with weight fluctuations, disordered eating, and body acceptance, I've always been able to hide my belly and thighs in regular-sized clothing and fool the world into thinking I'm smaller than I am. I firmly acknowledge that the body-positive movement belongs to the women and men who have never been able to hide their bodies under baggy tees and hip-hugging jeans and have experienced a lifetime of fat discrimination.

However, I would be remiss if I did not acknowledge that our fatphobic society affects every single one of us, causing many of us to practically kill ourselves to obtain a nearly unattainable body type while touting phrases such as "Nothing tastes as good as skinny feels," (thanks, Kate Moss) and "A moment on the lips, forever on the hips." And we would be remiss if we didn't admit that fatphobia, along with our Eurocentric "standards" of beauty, were both deliberate intentions of our white supremacist society to do everything in its power to put whiteness on the ultimate pedestal at our grave expense.

There isn't one person reading this book right now who hasn't struggled with trying to contort their body in some way, shape, or form to meet our society's extremely narrow, heavily biased, and barely attainable beauty standards. Barely attainable, because unless you're willing to go to extreme, life-threatening measures to meet these standards, you will never achieve them. Even those who are placed in the spotlight as "the standard" don't really look like *the standard*. Even the thinnest models aren't as thin as they appear to be when they walk a runway or appear on the cover of a magazine, because they have been photoshopped or altered in some way. Even those who are the standard aren't truly good enough. Yet we have all felt the immense pressure to make our bodies look like theirs. And more than likely, we've all tried some bodily or face-altering mechanism like Photoshop or waist-trainers to attempt to achieve that standard. (And if you haven't, you're a unicorn. And my daughters would like to meet you—they love unicorns.)

We've normalized (there's that word again) obsessing over the physical appearance of our bodies. We think this unnatural obsession over everything we believe is wrong with our body's appearance, and the demonizing and punishment we give ourselves as a result of that obsession, is somehow okay. We have been brainwashed by our society to believe we are so flawed that constantly berating and apologizing for ourselves has become our second language, oblivious to the deep, psychological self-harm this inflicts. The heartbreaking part is that we believe we deserve these critical words, thoughts, and self-hatred. The concept of unconditional self-love is so aberrant most of us can't even stand before the mirror and say "I love myself." Including me. Remember, I'm on this journey with you.

I find it deeply troubling that a society originally established to honor and protect the equality and value of humankind is a society that runs on its ability to get us all to hate ourselves. We are disposable to our society—only as good as the money we can deposit into the capitalist machine—and its greatest trick is to convince us that we are *disposable to ourselves,* so we continue to buy into the system. As we covered in chapter 3, capitalism is the engine that keeps white supremacy running—monetarily feeding the lies of human disposability and the gold standard of whiteness while making us even more disposable in the process. The beauty industry is one of the most effective ways this takes place, and we have all fallen for it. White supremacy culture has convinced us that if we just spend our lifetime obsessively altering our bodies and chasing that standard, one day we *might finally* get there.

So we spend our dollars chasing the latest trend we've been tricked into believing will finally make us less disposable (and maybe even worthy). Then that gold standard shifts ever so slightly (while still centering whiteness), making us do it all over again. As we run this rat race of chasing unattainable beauty, often in ways that are detrimental to our bodies, the standard continues to stay out of reach, and we continue to be dependent on whatever capitalism tells us we need to do next.

I was caught up in that vicious cycle. Unequivocally withering away as my weight dropped from 115 to 110 to 104 . . . 103 . . . I thought I was finally the epitome of beauty. When I looked in the mirror, I saw cheekbones I hadn't known existed. My clavicle protruded as the skin surrounding it sunk back. My arms and legs, once carrying pronounced muscles from years of tennis playing, became lanky stick-versions of themselves, perfectly parallel with the rest of my body as my natural, feminine curves slowly disappeared.

Finally, I thought to myself. *I'm finally skinny. I'm finally beautiful.*

Some days my only meal was a bowl of cereal, which was eaten out of desperation when I feared fainting from exhaustion and lack of fuel. But I oddly took pride in this. I was too busy to eat. Too involved in student government and the concert band at my university, among other activities, to make time for a proper meal. I wore my lack of time for eating and sleeping as a proverbial badge of honor—toting my busyness as a sign of status, importance, and the self-worth I had spent my life searching for. The less I ate and the less I slept, the more important I could make myself out to be. And the resulting heroine-like thinness that took over my body was the icing on the worthiness cake.

It was fake. The worthiness cake was fake. It was as if someone took icing and spread it over a cardboard cake look-alike and tried to convince me it was real. I loved how skinny I was, but I still hated my body. Anytime I ingested as much as a sip of water, my stomach ballooned with bloat, just like it had in middle school. My exhaustion was catching up to me, and I began making late-night McDonald's runs out of desperation to feed my body while running on triple shots of espresso to make it through my early morning classes. Daily migraines disrupted my life. And it was getting harder to hide the fact that I was purposefully not eating. This wasn't sustainable. I was hungry, and no matter how skinny my body looked, it still felt terrible.

I went from disordered eating to diving headfirst into what I thought was "healthy living," which was just diet culture's way of feeding the weight-loss obsession by sugarcoating it with the latest trend. And the trends were changing. The body-positive movement, which was started by fat, queer Black women, was co-opted by thin white women who were healing from eating disorders, and it went mainstream (as does everything co-opted by white women).[1] Starving yourself was out and so-called healthy eating was in. You know, kale smoothies and stuff. The marketing had a key directly to my soul because this latest trend spoke right to my desperation. I figured I could eat "clean" and finally *feel* better, hopefully get the flat stomach once and for all, and maintain the weight loss I had already "accomplished." And then, finally, finally, *finally* . . . I would have achieved "the standard."

But I never achieved the standard. The standard was created to never be achieved. The thinnest, blondest white woman will never be thin, blond, and white enough. There will always be something that doesn't measure up. There will always be some sort of imperfection that needs to be "fixed." There will always be a new trend that's placed ever so slightly higher than the last one so we can be fooled into believing it's within reach and worth chasing after. We will spend our lifetimes chasing these impossible beauty and body standards if we don't confront the lies of our white supremacy–rooted diet and beauty culture and disrupt the vicious cycle within ourselves.

How Thin and White Became the Standard

There was once a time in human history when the voluptuous, feminine curves that naturally hug a woman's body were revered. You can walk into any art museum and view artwork from the Renaissance era, and the eras surrounding it, that showcases soft ripples on a woman's belly, plump hips, and pronounced thighs. Such features represented a woman's fertility and femininity and honored the God-given design of her body without shame.[2] There have been periods of our history, such as the Paleolithic and Baroque eras, that placed fatness on a pedestal, as it represented wealth and prosperity.[3] A fat woman's body would be adorned in artwork and used in rituals intended to increase a woman's fertility.[4] Fatness was not feared.

There was once a time in human history when African, Asian, and Indigenous cultures were able to freely practice their own standards of beauty without regard for what European cultures depicted as *their* standards. White supremacy forces us to think history starts and ends in Europe, so when we look at the timeline of beauty standards throughout the historic eras, we often default to looking at it through a European lens. The Middle Ages, the Renaissance, the Victorian era . . . we are conditioned to believe that European eras are the center point of human existence. We learn about these eras as if they are the only ones that shaped our modern world, and as if cultures around the world automatically and voluntarily submitted to Western cultural leadership.

I find joy in the fact that nothing could be further from the truth. I love thinking about my African ancestors, and other Indigenous cultures alike, being able to mind their Black and brown business without being forced to submit to the fake authority of white supremacy and its beauty standards. European standards of beauty were just European standards of beauty . . . standards that were meant for the European body and only the European body. Every other culture around the world had its own depictions of what was considered "beautiful," and those depictions were based on traditional practices, wealth, marital status, age, religion, and more. Beauty was used to represent who you were and where you were in your life, depending on what was practiced within your culture. This doesn't mean that every single beauty standard before colonization was harmless. Patriarchy and misogyny existed long before colonization and white supremacy, and beauty standards, regardless of what culture they represented, were often rooted in both as they were typically set by men, enforced by men, and frequently coerced women into enduring painful practices to make themselves desirable *to* men.[5] Let's just go on the record right now and say that beauty should not have a standard to begin with.

However, that's another book. The point is, before colonization each culture of humans was free to exist in *their* culture, and set standards of beauty that honored *their* culture, without ever having to believe that their body was not good enough because it was not white or thin. Africans got to be African and practice African beauty. Asians were free to be Asian and practice Asian beauty. Indigenous peoples were free to be Indigenous and practice Indigenous beauty. And Europeans got to be European and practice European beauty. Whatever beauty meant to each culture, tribe, and ethnicity was what it meant. No believing that there is only one ideal of beauty that is beyond your reach because it exists in a body you could never obtain. No. Just freedom to be the person you were created to be, in the skin you were created to have, the curves you were created to carry, and the beauty rituals that paid homage to the culture that chose you.

Until whiteness took over. Until European Christians convinced themselves that *they* were the standard because their fair features "represented" the "light of God," intelligence, and every other "superior" attribute.[6] Until European Christians invaded the rest of the world and coerced everyone to heed to the fallacy that whiteness was equivalent to God-given superiority, dominion, and beauty. Until the emergence of anti-Blackness as a means to justify enslavement morphed into attaching the trait of fatness to Blackness to reestablish the blurring color lines as the population of persons deemed "part-Africanoid" was intensifying.[7] (I'll leave the cause of the increasing "mulatto" population up to the imagination. I'm sure you can connect the dots.)

Until white women were indoctrinated with the ideology that they must stay thin so that they never brought shame to the white race. Until every single physical feature that was associated with Blackness became the definition of disgrace, creating nearly an entire globe of people who would go to the most extreme measures just to get a little closer to whiteness.

———

We fear fatness because we fear Blackness. Read that again.

We fear fatness, darkness, and imperfection because we fear Blackness and have been brainwashed to associate those characteristics with Blackness. The natural curvature, deep hues, and prominent features that God intricately designed for the Black body became yet another thing race scientists used to fabricate Black inferiority and white superiority.[8]

Our round hips and luscious lips became the representation of laziness, greed, hypersexuality, and lack of intellect.[9] Our sun-kissed melanin became the equivalent of darkness, evil, and criminality.[10] Whiteness, placed on the altar of holiness and godliness, was fueled by the false Protestant ideology that whiteness was equivalent to God's favor, thus creating a dichotomy of lightness and darkness as the physical equivalents of beauty and ugliness. The church preached the message that white people must maintain religious, moral, and physical superiority by suppressing pleasure around food and exercising "self-control," because fatness was the result of the sin of gluttony.[11] Modern society has taken this fabricated narrative and run with it by placing it in every facet of societal marketing, from the first movies ever created that villainized the Black Mammy character, to Disney movies that included a dark, fat evil villain, to today's influencers selling you skinny teas on Instagram.

The ideology of white superiority predates colonization and enslavement. Remember what we learned in chapter 3: the belief

118

in whiteness as supreme and holy drove the behaviors of colonization, enslavement, and the construction of the institution of white
supremacy that we live within today. Before fatness was ever demonized, Blackness had long been viewed—by Europeans—as an
unsightly representation of insipidity.[12] Blackness was the marker
of the lowest social status and justifier of a lifetime of servitude to
whiteness.[13] (I made sure to add the disclaimer that these views
were held by Europeans, even though that's been well-established by
now, because I want it to be more than clear that Africans, people of
African descent, and People of Color have never voluntarily viewed
ourselves as abhorrent.)

When enslavement and colonization were in full force by the
sixteenth century, sugar was one of the primary crops harvested
and sold within the slave trade. Thus, an introduction to sugar and a
change in European diets and body figures emerged.[14] This brought
about the beginnings of fatphobia, primarily among elite European
men. Plump women were still revered, but fatness in men was seen
as evidence of a lack of self-control and intelligence—ideals produced by the Enlightenment era. This is the beginning of the belief
we still cling to: that self-regulation and withholding pleasure are
the keys to morality.[15]

With the negative connotations surrounding Blackness, the increase in enslavement and resulting mixed-race people, and scholars looking for as many reasons as possible to justify the racial
hierarchy, by the late seventeenth century we begin to see fatness
being associated with Blackness.[16] In the words of philosopher Jean-
Baptiste-Pierre Le Romain:

> Their penchant for pleasure makes them fairly unfit for hard labor,
> since they are generally lazy, cowardly, and very fond of gluttony. . . .
> They are lazy, drunken, gluttonous, and apt to steal.[17]

Such ideas only accelerated as time progressed. The more fatness was linked to Blackness, the more thinness was linked to whiteness.[18] European standards of beauty also changed from the seventeenth to the eighteenth centuries. The more fatness was associated with Blackness through race-based scientific literature, the more Europeans believed they needed to establish certain principles and rules of etiquette to control their "well-mannered" appearance within society. By the time we get to the nineteenth century and the rise of the American empire, magazines such as *Harper's Bazaar* and *Godey's Lady's Book* were preaching the narrative that thinness was the pinnacle of American beauty and exceptionalism.[19] It was also believed that showing restraint, or temperance, toward food and drink was ideal in the eyes of God. Obedience in this area would not only please God but ensure the physical evidence of racial superiority.[20]

And these are the ideals that have progressed for over a century to get us to where we are today. Deeply fearful of fatness. Deeply entrenched in chasing European standards of beauty. Believing so deeply in this narrative that we can't even see just how much harm it has caused us and continues to cause us.

Anti-Blackness and Anti-Fatness Today

The anti-Black and anti-fat narrative has become the very gospel we worship, infiltrating every institution within our society. Not only have we been coerced to bow down to its authority in the beauty industry but it has also become *the* premise for the standard of health in our medical system, serving as one of the main factors in determining eligibility for medical care.[21] The original agenda, of course, was to deter Black citizens from receiving proper treatment for ailments by using fatness as a blame factor and justification for denial of treatment.[22] Now the agenda still serves its original mission but has also become a multibillion-dollar weight loss and fat-shaming industry, using the premise of "health" to get people to buy into it without anyone realizing that the narrative they are being fed isn't necessarily the truth.

This narrative has even permeated our school system, preaching to children at young, impressionable ages that thin is equivalent to healthy and beautiful, using "fitness tests" and health education to begin the indoctrination of body shame before most kids even enter puberty. Our textbooks, strategically entrenched with majority white bodies as "examples," deliberately communicate the very clear message of who is superior.[23] This doesn't mean that learning about health and nutrition isn't important. It is. However, when it is taught in a biased, shameful, and inaccurate manner, it is no longer about wellness. It's fatphobia. It is discriminatory, shame-inducing fatphobia rooted in anti-Black stereotypes built on a foundation of racist lies. And when you preach any lie long enough, it will become accepted as fact. What began as a lie to prove Black laziness, gluttonousness, hypersexuality, and disease-ridden inferiority became a truism that nearly our entire world has held dear.

Here's the real truth: fatness is not based on your inability to control yourself. You are not morally superior the more "disciplined" you are around food. A thin body is not a more beautiful body, and a fat body is not a less beautiful body. You are not healthier if you are thinner or appear more "fit," and you are not unhealthier if you are what is considered "overweight" or "obese" via the very racist body mass index formula that takes zero consideration for genetics, underlying health conditions, environment, or ethnicity when it attempts to fit you into a narrow box of "health."[24]

Science has already proven that African American individuals tend to thrive at heavier BMIs than their white counterparts and that Asian people are at a higher risk for high blood pressure and diabetes even when they sit at a BMI comparable to what Americans consider "healthy."[25] Studies have already shown that the links between the Black community, higher BMIs, and comorbidities have much less to do with actual weight and everything to do with medical and systemic racism that has deliberately worked to deny proper care and a quality standard of living to Black Americans.[26] Fatphobia, fat discrimination, and so-called beauty standards have been proven time and time again to be rooted directly in white supremacy, racism, and *yes*, Protestantism. It has *been* time to disrupt this derogatory, harmful societal norm that has done nothing but cause every single one of us to hate ourselves, fear Blackness, and place whiteness on a pedestal it doesn't belong on.

But here's the thing—it's tempting to believe that all of this is behind us. After all, we're finally seeing more inclusive representation within beauty industry marketing. Women and men of all shapes and sizes are gracing our television screens and magazine covers. Clothing brands once notorious for catering to one specific body size and racial demographic have begun "diversifying" their marketing and clothing selection. And some of the models on the walls at Target actually have curves now. This is all a great start, but we are still a weight-obsessed, whiteness-chasing society. It has been ingrained into our brain waves to default to this behavior, and it's going to take much more than a few updated marketing campaigns to change that.

And if you look closely at those updated campaigns, you will still see that even among the latest trend of more inclusive beauty, whiteness and thinness are still favored. We are still more likely to see models with lighter skin than darker skin, and if there is dark-skinned representation, those models are held to much higher physical standards of beauty in other areas, such as facial features or thinness. We are still more likely to see thicker models with curves in "all the right places," such as the hips and butt, rather than the stomach and thighs. We rarely see a bloated model, a model with a face full of acne, or a model with a unibrow. We may see more natural hair, but preference is still given to looser curls, as it is assumed that looser equals a closer proximity to whiteness, rather than the tighter textures that are assumed to represent a closer proximity to Blackness. (Which is completely false, but I digress.)

We are still inundated with images of Kim Kardashian in her 2022 Marilyn Monroe Met Gala dress, which she bragged about losing sixteen pounds by only eating tomatoes to fit into, as her perfectly pronounced hourglass figure and curvaceous butt have become the representation of twenty-first-century beauty trends. Kim Kardashian is an example of how the beauty industry has now created a fetish of the very features Black women have spent centuries being demonized for. Yet these curvy features are only acceptable if we also maintain a thigh gap, flat stomach, and contoured face at all times. In other words, features that naturally grace many People of Color are only trendy when our whitewashed beauty industry says so, and only when those features are still glazed in whiteness.

Even with the so-called diverse representation and change in the latest ideal body type, many of us still look in the mirror and wish we could be smaller. We use filters on Instagram that apply Eurocentric features to our faces, like lighter eyes and a contoured nose, further imprinting the messaging that only *those* features are beautiful. Then we try following anti-diet culture and food-freedom influencers, hoping it will bring us closer to bodily liberation, yet wonder why we continue to compare ourselves to them. The truth is, even food-freedom influencers *still* uphold whiteness beauty standards themselves, as they are usually white women with small to midsize bodies that just so happen to have a little roll or cellulite on them. Don't get me wrong—this representation is important. Diet culture really had us believing that we were the only humans in the world with hip dips, belly rolls, and stomach protrusions. Yes, it's crucial that we're finally starting to see more normal bodies in our marketing, but when the only normal bodies we see are still considered "average" in size, as well as being either overwhelmingly white or lighter-skinned, this still places the standard and the norm right where it has always been—still "othering" and demonizing fatness, darkness, and anything that falls outside of the gender binary when it comes to the expression of beauty.

Even with the rise in inclusive representation, the vilification of fatness and Blackness has also increased in today's digital age. We are no longer able to just turn off the TV or walk away from that magazine and drown out the propaganda. Now we receive the message tenfold in the palm of our hands as it invades our social media feeds with ads for weight loss apps and influencers with lighter skin tones and toned tummies selling us detox smoothies. We don't realize it, but each time we see an image of society's standards flash before us, even if we think we are ignoring it, the messaging gets wired into our brains, which means we must work twice as hard to rewire our brains every single day. We can know everything there is to know about fatphobia, diet culture, and beauty standards being rooted in white supremacy and racism, yet they will still have a hold on us because they still run rampant in our culture.

To this day, I still look at myself in the mirror, suck my belly in, and wish my body could magically take the shape of the bodies I see dominating my Instagram page—one where the stomach is perfectly flat, the waist perfectly cinched, and the butt perfectly perched. To this day, I still grab my belly when I walk past a mirror, or when I bend over and it folds as it gives way to gravity, or after a meal that rightfully causes my belly to grow because I prioritized nourishment over physique. My body has taken on a much fuller size in recent years, as I have finally (mostly) healed my relationship with food, but it hasn't been a magical, overnight self-love party that is without difficulty. I have to remind my brain daily to view my body as fearfully and wonderfully made in all of its bends, folds, and protrusions, in spite of what society says. And while I've never been more in love with my milk chocolate skin, I still have days where I catch myself wishing my features were more Eurocentric.

———

I was in fifth grade when I got a relaxer in my hair for the first time. I'll never forget what the stylist said to me that day when I walked into her salon: "Do you want your hair nice and pretty and straight today?"

I looked up to see a beautiful, tall, slender Black woman with hair that danced like silk on her shoulders. She took my breath away. I had never seen a Black woman like me with white-people features . . . especially white-people hair.

"I guess?" I shrugged.

I was honestly confused. How was she going to make my hair straight? And why couldn't it be pretty the way it was? I mean, I knew the answer to the second half of that question. I'd known since I was in kindergarten that my hair wasn't what most would consider pretty. By the time I was in fifth grade, I was used to it. I just expected to never have pretty hair, to never be seen as "cute" or "hot" by the boys in my class, and to carry on for the rest of my life with one braid down the back of my head. I had no idea there was a way to alter my hair and make it look exactly like all of the white girls' hair I was jealous of in school and admired on television.

And I didn't know that the moment I looked at myself in the mirror after the stylist had finished and saw what I *could* look like was the moment I would begin chasing whiteness for years to come.

I could not stop brushing my hair. I mean, my brush actually ran through my hair! Like the white girls! I had seen them brush their hair and had never had that experience and finally, *finally*, I could brush mine too. That entire week, I walked with an extra swing in my step to force my hair to sway and swish as I walked. I practiced tucking my hair behind my ears just like the white girls did. Gosh, how I always wanted hair that tucked behind my ears. For the first time ever, the popular girls noticed me, and every other phrase said to me was, "Wow, Caroline, you should wear your hair like that all the time. It looks *so much better* straight."

I was beaming . . . beaming as the internal hatred I had for myself intensified almost overnight. The hairstyle lasted all of two weeks, and the closer I got to having to wash my hair and reveal my curls again, the more I hated the fact that I couldn't have just been born pretty . . . and white. If I had just been born white, I'd already have hair that was beautiful. I wouldn't have to go to the salon and spend hours and way too many dollars putting hair-altering chemicals and damaging heat on my tresses just to look like a white girl.

Then, just like that, it was over. For two weeks, I experienced life in closer proximity to whiteness just by straightening my hair. I experienced newfound attention and respect just by assimilating one of my physical characteristics from my natural Blackness to society's favored whiteness. And the only result from that superficially glorious two weeks was an even deeper hatred for myself, which had me frantically chasing whiteness just so I could *attempt* that feeling again.

It becomes a vicious cycle of addiction. You get one step closer to whiteness and experience the way our whiteness-centered society marvels at you while continuing to remind you that you'll never *quite* be there. You take all the fakeness off and look at the version you've been brainwashed to believe is ugly, and your self-worth plummets again. Your low self-worth leads to desperation, adding more fuel to the chase for whiteness, and you repeat. And let me clarify something: we are *all* chasing whiteness. Even if you're white. It looks different for each of us depending on our starting points within society, but each of us is chasing it. We just never realized it was whiteness we were chasing.

When I couldn't straighten my hair continuously, I became obsessed with makeup. All the white girls wore black, Avril Lavigne–inspired eyeliner, so I bought black eyeliner. All the white girls wore glitter eyeshadow, so I wore glitter eyeshadow. All the white girls wore Abercrombie & Fitch, so I begged my mom to let me wear Abercrombie & Fitch. Each time I assimilated to a trend, I experienced the cycle. Chasing the high that came with finally feeling like I could at least *resemble* those beauty standards, then coping with the crashing low that came each night when the eyeliner came off, the sweatpants went on, and I had to face my real body in the mirror. Lather, rinse, repeat.

Whiteness is not the standard. You are. *You* are the standard. Whatever state your body is in right now is *the standard.*

Thinness is not the standard.

Lighter skin is not the standard.

Straight, smooth hair is not the standard.

Thigh gaps are not the standard.

An hourglass figure is not the standard.

A flat stomach is not the standard.

Perfect skin is not the standard.

You get the picture.

The only standard that exists is you.

And I know some of this may sound cliché. Maybe even redundant, if you feel as though we're beginning to move past some of this harmful beauty and diet culture stuff, but it's not. Like I said before, a few marketing campaigns and a few influencers who are committed to breaking the narrative are not enough to disrupt the system of white supremacy that our entire beauty industry was founded upon.

As long as white supremacy remains in control, it will do what it was designed to do: retaliate against anything that goes against its authority with backlash that is always stronger than it has been before. For every body-inclusive swimsuit ad, there will be twice as many ads for weight loss programs. For every fat, Black, queer woman choosing to publicly celebrate her body, there will be thousands of hateful comments from people who still buy into the fatphobic and heteronormative narrative. And every time you choose to disrupt this narrative in your own life, self-deprecating doubtful thoughts will come rushing in, trying to trick you to fall back into that familiar place of believing your worthiness is tied to your ability to conform to the "standards."

Facing the societal and personal backlash is unavoidable, but now that you know the *root* of that backlash, you will be able to fight back. **You will finally be able to declare your liberation because you know exactly what you are liberating yourself from.** That is the key here.

I want to make it clear that beauty itself is not the enemy. Wanting to feel good about how you look is not the enemy. I think it's a very natural, human trait to want to love what you see in the mirror and use various techniques to accentuate the characteristics that God carefully placed on your body without mistake. You should find joy in however you choose to express the beauty you have been given without inhibition. It's one of the ways we show love and gratitude to the bodies God has given us.

So indulge in that skincare routine, deep condition your hair, exfoliate your skin, or try a new lipstick color. Or go makeup free, cut off all your hair, and wear that outfit you've always been told doesn't look good on your body. For my fellas reading this, get that fresh line-up, invest in that good razor, and yes, you exfoliate too! Dye your hair purple if you want to.

Or do absolutely nothing except look in the mirror and marvel at the beautiful human staring back at you. The creative expression of beauty itself is so liberating when we remove the pressure to chase a standard that was only ever created to deny us the worth we were born with.

And it's natural, and 100 percent okay, to want to feel optimally healthy and comfortable in your body, however that looks and feels to you. You have permission to do whatever you need to do to thrive in your body, but please know that your weight is never, ever connected to your beauty or worth as a human being. Please know that there is no shame in whatever form or size your body has chosen to take. Your body is working hard to keep you alive and needs every bit of its softness and strength to do so. Your body needs you to partner with it so that it can do what it was meant to do, and you can live the life you were meant to live.

Feed your body food that makes it *feel good* both physically and emotionally. Move your body in a way that makes it feel strong, alive, and liberated. Get to know the intricacies of your body, for you are the only advocate your body has. Your body is capable of so much on its own but relies on you every day to take care of it. Never stop handling yourself with care.

Remember this will be a daily battle. Have grace for yourself. It is okay to have those days when you want to give in and go back to that chase you know so well. But you're equipped with the truth now. You now know that everything you've been conditioned to believe about weight, beauty, and worth was created with an agenda to uphold the racial, social, and class structure of white supremacy in our society. Once again, it was never you. It was always them.

So embrace freedom from chasing a beauty standard ever again.

Journal Prompts

1. What did I learn about the beauty industry and the standards of whiteness that I didn't know before today? What surprised me about how white supremacy is so powerful that it even dominates the beauty industry?

2. What standards of beauty have I spent my entire life chasing? How has that chase impacted my self-worth?

3. How can I break up with the beauty standard chase? What do I currently struggle with? What part of me do I still wrestle with seeing as beautiful in its natural state?

4. How do I need to heal from the lies of beauty culture? What is making this healing difficult?

6

Hustle

You have the same amount of hours in one day as they do, Caroline.
There are no excuses.

Hi there. Welcome to my brain, where one primary thought has
existed for the majority of my life: *There are no excuses. If they can do*
it, so can you. ("They" meaning Beyoncé, that influencer with a six-
figure business, or my college classmate who didn't have children to
care for.) I expected myself to perform at a capacity others perform
at but are only able to because they have more or different resources
available to them.

This is such a toxic mindset, but I didn't know it at the time. I was
a newish mom to a two-year-old and a newborn, and I thought I
had it all figured out. I had spent the first year of my firstborn's life
figuring out how to perfect a routine so that I could optimize my
time and get more done without letting motherhood "get in my way."
I firmly believed that we all have the same twenty-four hours in a
day as Beyoncé, or anyone else who has achieved great success in
life, and the only thing holding us back from success was ourselves
and our excuses. There were a lot of other productivity coaches and

131

books to back me up on this, so I never once thought about how harmful, ableist, and patriarchal this messaging was.

By the time my second daughter was about eight months old, I even started a business around this concept to teach other mothers how to get their sense of productivity back after entering motherhood. I'd spent nearly every moment after my second daughter's birth trying to perfect our new routine so that I could still somehow function at the same level of productivity I was able to execute before having kids.

I was not willing to allow being a mother to halt my lifelong rat-race pursuit of success. No, no, no. Motherhood would not be an excuse for not starting a business while working full-time, maintaining my daily 5:00 a.m. fitness routine, keeping the house spotless, cooking dinner every night, running errands, attending playdates, driving my stepson to all of his activities, and being a devoted wife. All I needed was a routine and the right #bossmode mentality. Not succeeding was not an option. My time and my life were my responsibility. If I wanted success in all areas of my life, then I needed to put in the work. No. Excuses.

And if I could do it, you could do it too. I'd be there to teach you how. I didn't use the word *hustle* per se, but that's exactly what I was teaching. Just in mom-speak. Hustle culture, but for moms. #momboss.

Oh, the toxicity! I'm cringing at my past self. But it gets worse. When the novel coronavirus first entered our world in 2020 and forced us into a monthslong lockdown, I figured it was the perfect time to up the intensity and tell everyone else to do the same. Now there really was no excuse. No outside obligations, no commutes, no events. Just all the time in the world to crush all the goals, do "all the things," and show the rest of the world what we mothers were made of. I was anti-negativity, anti-complaining about life or motherhood being too hard, anti-resting, and of course, anti-excuses. I'm embarrassed to admit that I looked down on anyone who used the unpredictability of life as an excuse to not be a productive human being.

I'm disgusted that this was my former mentality, but I was nothing but a product of the culture that surrounded me. The culture that surrounds all of us. The culture that has bred a deep obsession with performance (in every aspect) because of the brainwashing we have endured from white supremacy culture that tells us our performance is equivalent to our worth as a human.

You know the theme by now. This is chapter 6, after all. We are so addicted to productivity that even when the entire globe entered an unprecedented health crisis, people were tweeting and posting that we should all be using this time to pursue that goal or chase that dream we'd been putting on hold. If we didn't, we could no longer use time as an excuse for our lack of accomplishment in life. If we couldn't get it done during a forced quarantine, then a lack of time was never the problem in the first place. The problem was *us*.

I saw people comparing the opportunities for increased productivity to how Shakespeare wrote *King Lear* during a plague.[1] If Shakespeare could do that in the sixteenth century (when people had no electricity, running water, or mandate to stay home), then we had no excuse for not using this time to launch that side hustle, start that podcast, write that book proposal, or dive headfirst into homeschooling our kids with perfection as if we had been doing it all along. Never mind the fact that life as we knew it changed within a literal blink of an eye. Never mind the fact that we were in the midst of a global crisis with no end in sight. Never mind the fact that we were walking through collective trauma and witnessing higher amounts of global death and disease than ever before while one of our primary human needs for connection was replaced with mandatory isolation. Somehow, we were still expected to magically produce the next life-changing innovation or *New York Times* bestseller—while our bodies went into survival mode, begging us for rest.

I don't think there has ever been a time in recent human history that has been more evident of our prioritization of profit over people than during the first two years of the COVID-19 pandemic. It has taken an entire pandemic to expose the truth about the sheer brokenness and toxicity of capitalism and how deeply detrimental it is that the livelihood of our society relies on it.

<hr />

Forget about the productivity-during-lockdown mentality for just a second and take a hard look at the reality of how our society responds to labor crises. The concerted efforts to preserve the wealth of the (mostly) white elite by creating an economy that depends on the exploitation of the labor of marginalized communities means our economy runs on the backs of majority Black and brown people and their so-called unskilled labor. We have been taught to abhor "unskilled" workers as if laziness is the only reason they find themselves in those positions. Society has given them this offensive title of "unskilled," which couldn't be further from the truth, considering every job requires skill, hard work, and, in most cases, the ability to withstand subpar working conditions.

It is the exploitation of the term *unskilled* that has served as justification for those poor conditions and corresponding low wages. Low-wage workers are the real "hustlers" in our society, without whom our way of life would not stay afloat. The pandemic prompted a title upgrade for many in classically low-wage industries like retail and food production to "essential workers," along with those in the medical field.[2] So they continued on with a few performative nods of respect from those of us who were privileged enough to work comfortably from our homes while hoarding toilet paper from Costco.

Toilet paper we wouldn't have without our essential workers in the first place. However, that newfound "respect" didn't increase their wages. Those few public thank-yous didn't protect them from being disproportionately impacted by the severity of COVID-19.

At a time when lives should have mattered more than profit, profit *still* trumped humanity as the truth behind the structure of our white supremacist, capitalist economy was finally revealed for all to see: it is the most marginalized, most disregarded, and lowest-earning population that keeps our economy afloat. And we were finally able to prove that it's the system, not the people themselves, that has purposefully placed our communities of color, predominantly, in those positions to be marginalized, underserved, underpaid, overworked, and as a result, most heavily impacted by almost every single crisis our society faces.

The Truth about Hustle Culture

We have been led to believe that our obsession with work, productivity, racing to the top, and chasing six figures (also known as hustle culture) stems from the infamous false pretense of capitalism that we can be anything we want to be if we just work hard enough. Just like every other message society screams at us, this one comes at us from every angle. As we discussed in chapter 4, it begins in the classroom when we are interrogated about our future career aspirations before we even know how to read. As we get older, the message continues as we are constantly drilled about our grade point averages and nonnegotiable collegiate goals. Once we enter adulthood, the message gets louder as we're bombarded with every MLM scam and pressured to start a business to create multiple revenue streams, hustle our way to the top of our corporate careers, and get that second or third degree while we're at it. Everyone seems to have their own rags-to-riches story, and if they can do it, we can do it too, right? Just hustle hard enough, and you can be anything you want to be in the land of opportunity.

This is not the true root of hustle culture.

Now, there isn't one specific definition of hustle culture, but the gist of it is that it's an over-glorification of work.[3] While the term *hustle culture* only materialized within the last decade or so, the concept itself is nothing new. It has been the oxygen of our society since the plantation days. The true roots of hustle culture stem from our white supremacist society creating capitalism to secure wealth and power for the white elite by exploiting the labor of the Black community (read: enslavement, sharecropping, domestic work, and so on), and later all marginalized communities. The evidence of this is clear: our lowest-wage workers, who are disproportionately BIPOC and disabled, struggle with things like housing and food insecurity while doing the *essential work* that keeps our economy afloat. Essential work that *requires* hustling. Meanwhile, the rest of society has bought into the lie that meritocracy will save us from being "stuck" in the lower class, so we wear our obsession with hustling as a badge of honor.

(Reminder: meritocracy is the belief that people get ahead in society based on their merit, or accomplishments, rather than their social class. However, as we have learned, white supremacy has created an illusion of meritocracy by building systems that ensure the progress of the white middle and upper classes by withholding progress from People of Color, primarily Black people, and lower classes.)

The meritocracy myth is what justifies our obsession with work, status, class, and wealth, as well as our disregard and disdain for the poor. We are taught that every aspect of our lives falls solely on us and is directly correlated to our work ethic. We are taught to view those who need help as weak or lazy. If they "just worked hard enough," they wouldn't be in a position to need help in the first place. It is this toxic culture that enables us to survive off the backs of low-wage workers, continuing to happily feed the system that was designed to fail us all, while simultaneously looking down on anyone we think is beneath us. The toxicity. The entitlement. The audacity.

When I began to do the inner work of dismantling white supremacy culture within myself, my obsession with hustle culture was, and still is, the hardest to divest myself from. I've mentioned in almost every chapter that I spent most of my life believing that pushing myself to the brink in the name of hard work was the key to my success and self-worth. Hustle mentality has been the characteristic of white supremacy culture I fully embodied without question. I can't put my finger on it, but *something* made me question every other aspect of what I now know as white supremacy culture even though I still allowed myself to fall in line with all of it. I secretly questioned why, as a culture, we were so obsessed with being thin, but I still fell in line with that obsession. I secretly questioned why, as a culture, we believed that whiteness is the standard of beauty, but I still bought into that ruthless lifestyle.

However, I never once questioned our addiction to never-ending work and our contempt for any sort of rest. I fell for it in high school, fully convinced that the less I slept and the harder I worked, the more successful and worthy I would become. I fell even deeper for it in college, diving into the #teamnosleep mentality, nearly driving myself insane while effectively giving myself chronic anxiety. I never questioned the anxiety and exhaustion I had grown accustomed to because the productivity gurus made it clear that these symptoms were part of my worthiness requirements. I never questioned my belief that so-called hard work would make me morally superior to anyone who appeared as though they didn't work as hard as I did.

(That is to say, I turned my nose up at anyone who didn't have a college degree or wasn't on track to get one.) I never questioned the narrative openly taught by society that anyone of a lower class, or poor status, must have gotten there on their own accord and that if they had just worked harder they wouldn't be such a "drain on society." (Again, I'm cringing at my past self but also cringing at our collective lack of empathy.)

I never questioned it because it was *normal*. Burnout, exhaustion, anxiety, and a resulting morally superior attitude are not only normal but *encouraged*. Encouraged so that the capitalist engine can keep the white supremacy machine running without a hitch. It quietly hums along and performs its duties as we all fall prey to its harm that disguises itself as success.

The more we are brainwashed to believe that capitalism's toxic, harmful ideologies are normal and positive, the more it thrives. And the continued success of white supremacy relies on capitalism's ability to thrive.[4] These systems work together, depending on one another to keep the machine going. I like to think of the characteristics and ideologies of whiteness (see the list from chapter 3 as well as the subcultures we've discussed in this book) as the currency the systems breed. Like an ATM, we receive the currency from the machine, spend it among ourselves to keep the energy flowing, and deposit it back into the machine to keep it running. Since, as humans, we are naturally drawn to currency, we believe it is something to be valued, chased, and invested in. So we do just that. We invest in that currency, whatever ideology it may be (individualism, beauty culture, perfectionism, and so forth), and it grows exponentially, causing nothing but harm.

In this case, *hustle culture* is one of the main currencies the white supremacy machine has given us to idolize, spend, and invest. The capitalist engine absolutely cannot run if its constituents aren't obsessed with or reliant upon its very reason for existence: amassing wealth and power. Wealth and power cannot be funneled into and hoarded by the elite class if there are no lower classes to do most of the work with the false hope of reaping benefits they will never see. But all we see is that false hope. We see that glimmer of the potential of what *could be* while being unrelentingly persuaded that our entire destiny is at the mercy of our own merit. So we build an altar of worship to the god of hustle with the hope of grabbing just a fraction of that glimmer. Or we build that altar out of force, knowing good and well that wealth will likely never be ours and praying that our hustle is enough to put food on the table every night. Either way, we all fall victim to worshiping the god of hustle whether we realize it or not. Again, this is not our fault. This is society doing exactly what it was created to do.

American Capitalism: It All Started on the Plantation

It's true: American capitalism began right on the plantation.[5] Many would credit the Industrial Revolution as the beginning of American capitalism, but I would argue that the Industrial Revolution was what, for lack of a better word, *revolutionized* capitalism and solidified its permanence. The plantation laid the groundwork for capitalism. It introduced America to what was possible and allowed America to perfect the system to ensure its success.

Slavery has been ruled by riches since the beginning. This is nothing new. Remember, that's what drove the Portuguese to voyage down the coast of West Africa for themselves. They wanted to see what riches the Africans had that they thought rightfully belonged to them because they believed Africans were too brutish to deserve such treasure.

Fast-forward to the height of the transatlantic slave trade, and planters, the elite, and governing leaders discovered just how much money they could make from selling cotton overseas and also re-alized the monetary value of their enslaved property. Cotton be-came our nation's most valuable export and the world's most traded commodity, and the combined value of every enslaved person was greater than all of the railroads and factories in the country.[6]

If it wasn't for the cotton industry, the New York Stock Exchange and Wall Street (built by the enslaved, by the way) would not have been founded.[7] As soon as white elites realized the monetary value and trading potential of cotton, they began placing investments in cotton, which turned it into an industry. Those investments, along with direct profits made by selling cotton to England and investing in enslaved persons themselves, funneled money into the economy, leading to the almost overnight accumulation of wealth not only for the plantation owners and white elite but the nation.

This solidified the culture of procuring wealth by any means necessary, especially by *exploiting the labor of those beneath you*. This was the beginning of adding wealth and economic status to the defi-nition of white superiority.

This was the beginning of American capitalism.

Present-Day Capitalism: Lonely Workaholism

One of the key characteristics of hustle culture is performative workaholism, often to the point of burnout. But as we said before, there are two faces of hustle culture: the one that breeds performa-tive workaholism and an obsession with burning the midnight oil to prove your self-worth and chase society's materialistic, entitled definition of success, and the one that is forced onto the members of our society who cannot reasonably afford to live safely and com-fortably in our economy *without hustling*. Sometimes, our hustle may be a bit of both.

The first hustle culture may present itself as the normalized behavior of answering your boss's email at 3:00 a.m., taking your laptop to your family vacation on the beach, working longer than your expected hours for no overtime pay just so you can appear as committed as possible, and ignoring vital human needs such as proper nutrition, exercise, community, and sleep just to cram a few more hours of work into your day. That performative work, of course, is not complete without a glorified, aesthetically pleasing picture on Instagram that proves just how busy and important you are and gives you a temporary high of feeling good about all that you've accomplished. The second face of hustle culture may present itself in having no choice but to work multiple jobs or constantly seek overtime work just to keep food on the table or afford more than just paying your bills (and to hope that overtime work will eventually lead to some sort of promotion so you can breathe a little).

Both sides of hustle culture feed off of each other, are the direct result of white supremacy, and contribute to our diminishing self-worth as we continue to receive the loud message that we will never be good enough no matter how hard we push ourselves.

So . . . I recently started getting into TikTok. It's become my guilty pleasure. When it first hit the social media scene, I swore up and down I'd never download the app. I also said the same thing when Instagram first debuted. An app where you just share pictures of yourself? Why would I do that there when I was already doing that on Facebook? I also had reservations about Facebook when it was introduced to the high school crowd circa 2005.

Okay, okay . . . I've always had reservations about joining the latest trends. But, just like Facebook and Instagram made their way into my world, TikTok has too. And I quickly was hooked. I thought

TikTok was just for teenagers trying to prove to strangers on the internet that they can dance. I was wrong. TikTok has become the place where I learn the most fascinating information about our world and the beautiful humans living in it. Yes, it's also hilarious. If you need a good laugh, head to TikTok and prepare for your insides to hurt. And yes, people dance and it's way more entertaining to watch than I expected it to be.

But people also get on TikTok to educate others, spread awareness about important issues, and talk about their life experiences, whether these be about growing up in a non-white household, working for an underserved school district, or living as an expat in a different country. As I've watched hundreds of videos of people sharing their vastly different life experiences, I've come to one conclusion: white supremacy has a hold on all of us. No matter how different or extraordinary the stories are, each has the common thread of white supremacy culture woven through it.

If there's one thing to know about TikTok, and all social media for that matter, it's that it operates in *trends*. What's trending, or what everyone is talking about at the moment, is always the primary focus of social media. I've noticed a particular TikTok trend lately that has caught my attention: immigrants or exchange students sharing the culture shocks they faced when coming to America. Many people are downright stunned when they experience the hurried hustle culture of the American way of life and struggle to make connections with others because of the *individualism* that we've normalized.

(Remember, individualism *is a primary characteristic of white supremacy culture, and it's one of the dominant characteristics that allows hustle culture to prosper.)*

They find that American culture is lonelier, less healthy both physically and mentally, and places value in money when much of the non-white-dominated world places value in community and family.

This is what the exploitation of marginalized labor, justified by capitalism's individualistic "your lack of success is your fault" messaging that breeds the glorification of performative workaholism, has done to us. We are left with an overburdened, lonely society that is in desperate need of real community. We're exhausted, drained, and honestly just plain miserable.

The Truth behind the Hard Work Mindset

Now, this is one of the chapters where you may experience the most resistance or defensiveness to what I've presented. After all, having a strong work ethic has been infused into our DNA as the number one characteristic one can possess that will "guarantee" success and right standing in our society, and to some degree this is true. Plus, a strong work ethic is an honorable characteristic to have. This is not an argument against that.

Many of you, myself included, are able to look back on your life and see evidence of your hard work paying off in some socially glorified way, whether that be earning a degree, getting a promotion at your job, or spending hours upon hours writing a book that you pray becomes a bestseller (wink, wink). I say "socially glorified" not to diminish the accomplishments themselves—because they are wonderful and you should be proud of them—but because they are the *main types* of accomplishments that get the "society verified" checkmark of approval. The degrees, promotions, fancy job titles, and any other achievements that can be measured with some sort of verifiable metrics tend to be the only achievements that society deems worthy of recognition and that make us "worthy" as human beings. They also tend to be accomplishments that can only be achieved by willingly submitting to the authority of hustle culture. You don't get the degree or the fancy job title by putting in an appropriate amount of work with a healthy balance of meeting human needs outside of said work. You get it by putting in the extra hours, surviving on four hours of sleep and four shots of espresso, making yourself available at every waking hour or going above and beyond your job description without appropriate compensation.

This is the kind of "hard work" that society uses as proof to be able to say, "See? Hard work is all you need to be successful," while conveniently ignoring the fact that it is practically killing us from every angle, whether it be burnout from the romanticized success-chasing or the substandard working conditions that purposefully withhold meeting needs that no human should ever have to do without. The more we fall for it, the more we ignore the *real truth* that specific systems have been built to keep certain levels of society-approved success away from certain demographics. White supremacy continues to effectively carry out its mission, and our willful ignorance enables the mission and ensures its victory.

Nevertheless, it is the capitalist-bred hard work mentality that has dubbed Western society as the *land of opportunity,* and with good reason. To a certain extent, capitalism grants us nearly endless opportunities to do or be anything we want to. If you wanted to start a business tomorrow, you could go online, register an LLC in your state, and be in business within minutes. If you decided you wanted to go back to school, you could easily find a school that fits your needs and apply for admission within just a few hours. In both cases, if you're willing to "work hard," then technically you should be "successful" with your endeavors. Obviously, a successful business and completion of a degree won't come to you if you sit on your butt all day. We know that. Regardless, working harder won't get you very far if you also have to work three jobs just to make tuition payments or if racial discrimination keeps you from getting a business loan or if you still can't afford childcare no matter how many extra gigs you take on, so you're forced to put your endeavors on hold yet again.

Hard work won't bring you true satisfaction if you have to burn yourself out just to meet a baseline requirement for whatever it is you are pursuing, forcing you to halt your journey and toss your progress out the window because now your health is suffering. Hard work certainly won't get you anywhere when you hustle yourself to the bone in a blue-collar position only to receive a raise that is laughable, get passed over for a promotion you more than deserve, and still have to take on a second job because your wages don't reflect the rising inflation rates.

———

The issue here is not with the concept of working hard or the accomplishments that quality hard work can bring. Hard work, on its own, is a desirable and God-honoring characteristic that, when exercised intentionally, can yield abundant fruit. The issue here is the way white supremacy culture has redefined hard work and weaponized it by attaching it to our worth as human beings while conveniently ignoring all of the barriers to entry white supremacy itself has built to ensure that no amount of hard work will ever amount to "success," as defined by white supremacy culture, for the majority of the population.

Hard work should not be defined as *ignoring every aspect of your human needs to focus solely on work and nothing else to either relentlessly pursue wealth and power or to merely survive in this economy,* yet this is the definition that white supremacy culture has forced upon us by doing exactly what it was constructed to do. Because white supremacy exists for the sole purpose of keeping elite, white, and mostly Christian-identifying men in positions of power and wealth in our society, the systems that have been built to keep that power and wealth away from primarily BIPOC communities have, over time, made it nearly impossible for the average person to experience the so-called success capitalism has promised us. But, again, that promise has us brainwashed, so we believe that not only is it still possible to eventually reach that standard we have been chasing but it is something *worth* chasing. We are caught in the trance of the idol we have made of hustle, success, and achievement, which allows us to think that sacrificing our humanity, no matter how detrimental that sacrifice is, is worth it.

It will never be worth it. Ever. There is no amount of success, wealth, or power for which it is ever worth sacrificing the very human needs God created you to have. It is never worth it to deny yourself rest, food, drink, fun, love, pleasure, joy, or human connection just to chase a narrow version of "success" that exists to exploit others in the first place. Sacrificing your humanity will not make you more worthy, make you morally superior, fulfill whatever it is you think it will fulfill, or give you the freedom you think it will. And it doesn't necessarily guarantee you the success you've been told it will bring you, either. All that is guaranteed as a result of that sacrifice, besides *maybe* being able to afford extra guac on your Chipotle, is extreme burnout, health complications, damaged relationships, mental health that is on the fritz, tanked self-worth, and the continued glorification of white supremacy culture that just keeps the cycle going.

And there is never any human need that should ever have to go unmet just because the appropriate amount of labor the human body was created to withstand still isn't enough to provide those needs. Needs like adequate shelter, consistent food sources, reliable transportation, and time to rest are not luxuries, yet in our society they are treated as such—only reserved for those who are either fortunate enough to sit in positions of privilege due in part to the exploitation of marginalized labor, or who have accepted a fate of forever hustling, sacrificing the very needs they are hustling just to be able to meet.

Hustle Culture Will Always Catch Up to Us . . .

It was the year 2000. I was sitting in my living room, watching my then-favorite show on my favorite network, *7th Heaven* on the WB. During a commercial break, the WB announced a new show that was coming to the network about a single mother and her teenage daughter. I remember sitting there in jaw-dropping awe as I watched snippets of this duo who acted much more like best friends than mother and daughter. I immediately fell in love—tuning in every Tuesday night to watch a relationship that I dreamed of experiencing with my daughter one day. I saw a mother who enjoyed and trusted her teenage daughter and a teenage daughter who seemed free to be herself without fear, ridicule, or pressure to conform to anyone's standards, especially her mother's. *Gilmore Girls* quickly replaced *7th Heaven* and has been my favorite TV show ever since.

The mother, Lorelai, had gotten pregnant at sixteen, dropped out of high school, ran away from home, and raised her daughter in a small town about thirty minutes from where she grew up. Her daughter, Rory, was now sixteen—the same age her mother was when she became pregnant with her. Rory was incredibly smart, a bookworm, loved to study, and dreamed of attending Harvard. She made being a nerdy bookworm cool, which is exactly what I needed at that moment of my adolescence. Lorelai, who spent her childhood crushed under the weight of unrelenting pressure and high expectations placed on her by her parents, had been a much more rebellious teenager. Rebellion was her response to her parents' attempt to force her to conform to what they believed to be the only acceptable version of a human being. Her parents were exceptionally wealthy and only measured success the way society has conditioned us to: an Ivy League degree, wealth, marriage, status, and class. They turned their noses up at anyone who worked in blue-collar positions, didn't attend an Ivy League school, and wasn't what they would call a "productive member of society." And having a child out of wedlock? As a teenager? Oh, you can forget it. An immediate embarrassment to the family's "upstanding reputation."

Essentially, they were white supremacy culture, personified. They were exactly who our society was built for: wealthy white families who procured their wealth off the backs of chattel slavery and passed it on to the next generations who were able to build upon that wealth because the system was created to ensure their ability to do so—while basking in the guaranteed success that their wealth and privilege granted them and passing it off as "merit."

Lorelai chose to redefine the definition of success she had been fed her entire life. She didn't fit into the pretentious Ivy League box her parents tried to force her into and spent the majority of her childhood planning her escape from that world. Instead of taking what would have been handed to her via her parents' wealth and class privilege, she chose to start from the "bottom" of a career in a blue-collar position and work her way up to a career level that felt right for her, never believing for a moment that she was less than just because her career status (and teenage single parenthood) would suggest otherwise to the likes of society (and her parents.)

(Note: I don't like referring to blue-collar positions as the "bottom," because that's exactly the mentality we need to divest ourselves from, but for the sake of context, I used the term to best illustrate Lorelai's story.)

She didn't hustle by ignoring her personal needs or the needs of her daughter to work her way up in her field. She sowed and tended exactly where she was at each stage, taking delight in the season she was in, enjoying and embracing what was in front of her, finding the beauty in it all, and never wavering in how she viewed herself. She took the exorbitantly high standards and expectations of her parents' world and tossed them right out the window, choosing to believe that success could be achieved right where she was, at the pace she felt called to. (If only it was this easy for us in the real world to do the same.) And while Rory had her sights set on attending an Ivy League school and pursuing a career in journalism, her passion for those things was not driven by a need to prove herself worthy to society but rather came from within, and her drive came from watching her mother value hard work in a way that wasn't attached to worth but to *purpose*.

Now, this story isn't perfect. White supremacy culture is never fully escapable unless we are actively divesting ourselves from it daily. And obviously, the character Lorelai wasn't written as trying to separate herself from white supremacy culture, as there was no mainstream knowledge of its existence in the early 2000s. All that Lorelai knew was that something about the way she was raised, and the entitlement her parents were mercilessly proud of possessing, didn't sit well with her, and she wanted to raise her child differently.

I think that's quite common among many of us and has been for decades. Many of us have been able to discern that something wasn't quite right with the way our society operates—we just didn't know how to properly articulate exactly what the problem was, nor did we have an accurate understanding of it. Because this is our culture, we're taught that these systems are the "correct" way of doing things, and even if we don't fully buy it, we think we don't have a choice but to comply. Many of us may have attempted, like Lorelai, to escape certain aspects of the culture without fully grasping that it's the *entire system* we need to divest ourselves from. When we attempt to only escape certain aspects of a harmful system while either willingly or unknowingly staying within the system as a whole, we never truly escape. It will always catch up to us.

Gilmore Girls is the perfect example of how the system eventually caught up to both Lorelai and Rory, with hustle culture getting the best of them. Rory wanted to attend a prep school so that she could increase her chances of getting into Harvard. The fact that she felt the need to attend an expensive, "prestigious" prep school just to better her chances of getting into an expensive, "prestigious" university is white supremacy culture at work right there.

First of all, remember that the idea of what is prestigious is merely the attitudes and behaviors of the white elite who decided for the rest of the world that their way of living was superior to everyone else's. Just because an educational institution is old, has historic European architecture, focuses only on a Eurocentric curriculum with standards that are practically beyond human, and charges three times the average salary just to obtain that education doesn't make it prestigious. Second of all, the fact that you have to pay hundreds of thousands of dollars to receive an education that *might* better your chances of getting into a so-called prestigious university that also costs hundreds of thousands of dollars is all the proof you need to demonstrate exactly who "success" in our society is reserved for. In most cases, the myth of meritocracy continues, as many students who are admitted into these presumedly distinguished schools are only admitted because of who they know and how much money they have.

Rory's grandparents were well-connected with the headmaster of the prep school she attended, and it was their money that paid for her tuition at both the prep school and, later, Yale University, which was where her grandfather happened to attend. See the pattern? Yes, Rory was an excellent student and put forth tremendous effort toward her studies, but at the end of the day she used the advantages of the very world her mother ran away from to obtain her titles of success.

However, even with those advantages, which the majority of the students at her school benefitted from (most parents were rich and well-connected to ensure their son or daughter's academic success whether they deserved it or not), the culture of the prep school was the epitome of hustle culture. They demanded perfection. Humanity was never allowed to show its face. The students were all under exorbitant amounts of pressure, which showed up as anxiety, bullying, being willing to go to extreme and unethical measures just to get an A, and overexerting themselves to participate in extracurricular activities and community service just to be able to put it on their résumés. At one point, Rory freaks out about not having enough volunteer work on her transcript and wants to "Find a r——d kid and teach him how to play softball."[8] Not only did she use incredibly offensive and ableist language, but her hustle was utterly performative.

Even though Lorelai never forced Rory to define success the way society conditions us all to do, society's conditioning still made its way into Rory's mind. Sure, she still had a genuine passion for education, but because her society had certain rules all must adhere to in order to achieve certain things, regardless of reason, she was still coerced into that performative hustle culture. And that coercion not only resulted in a tremendous amount of mental harm but a continued complicity in the system that slowly took over, causing an innocent, passionate bookworm to morph into a self-absorbed, entitled, burned-out young adult. We re-meet Rory at age thirty-two in the *Gilmore Girls: A Year in the Life* reboot, and she has completely stalled out in the very career she'd invested an exorbitant amount of money, time, and mental health into receiving an education for. While fictional, Rory's story is an example of how white supremacy culture, and more specifically hustle culture, always catches up to us.

... If We Don't Divest Ourselves from It

Let me make one thing clear: I am in no way dismissing the need for humans to work or even the importance of hard work. I am also not dismissing the need for education to do the majority of the work required to sustain our livelihood and our economy. God created us to work. God created us to do good, meaningful, intentional work on his earth so that we can serve each other, provide for ourselves, and cultivate the land he has entrusted to us. God created humans to use their knowledge and talents to create a living and care for one another.[9]

Our very livelihood depends on work—not only because we are forced to work in exchange for an income that we may or may not be able to survive on but because without any work, we physically would not be able to meet our basic human needs. And the majority of the work we do requires education, training, and development to perform to the best of our ability. We know this.

Someone has to work for our bodies to receive the food, clothing, and shelter they need. Someone has to work for us to have doctors to see when we are sick or lawyers to hire when we need legal assistance. Someone has to work for me to use a computer to type this manuscript. Someone has to work for this manuscript to become the book you are holding in your hands.

And someone has to provide an education for almost every kind of work that we do. This is all meaningful, intentional, humanity-serving work that the fall of humankind caused us to lose sight of.

(If "fall of humankind" doesn't resonate with you, replace that with "greed and love of power," which have caused us to lose sight of the humanity-focused work that it is in our biological nature to do.)

It was never supposed to be this way.[10] And I know that we know there is no way we can just hear a few sermons, snap our fingers, and pray for the world to come to its senses and return to God's original design for us. We know that total redemption will come only when Jesus himself returns. We know that a euphoric society of world peace is impossible to obtain because, no matter what we do, evil will still exist.

However, we cannot use that as an excuse to not do anything. God has called us to do his radical redemptive work in the world while we wait for his return. Jesus set the example for this when he walked the earth, performed his ministry, and boldly fought systems of oppression and injustice, which led to his execution.[11]

Greed, pride, fear, and hate have led to the construction of this white supremacist society that we are all living in and have been indoctrinated by. However, we often want to address the personal heart issues without addressing the fact that an entire society was constructed as a result of those heart issues, or "flaws" that "a few of our leaders happened to possess." A society that impacts every single person, regardless of faith, ethnicity, race, or gender identity.

Jesus never told the poor that if they just "hustled harder" they would no longer be poor. He never told the oppressed that if they just proved themselves to be like those who were in power, they would no longer be oppressed. He never once told anyone in his ministry that they were not worthy unless they worked themselves to the bone to achieve narrow standards set by those in the highest positions of power at that time. No. He denounced the structures that those in power created, especially those who used religion as a basis for their creation. He worked to restore equity, equality, humanity, and liberation that those destructive systems of oppression stole.[12] I firmly believe that if he were walking the earth today, he would be actively working to destroy the most powerful system of oppression that has existed since his execution, and I believe even more firmly that he has called us to take that work we are burying ourselves with, in the name of hustle culture, and use it instead to dismantle these systems that have stolen so much from all of us.

<hr />

Normally, at the end of a chapter, I remind you of how much you're worth and that the standards you have been expected to uphold are no longer your burden to bear. I tell you what you can do personally to divest from these systems and rewrite a narrative for yourself that only serves your healing and liberation. The same, of course, is true here, because as I've mentioned before, you cannot begin to dismantle the oppressive systems within society without divesting yourself from them first. Since none of us can fully separate ourselves from our capitalistic society (unless you want to isolate yourself on a self-sustaining compound somewhere far, far away or move to a non-capitalist country), in this case, this means breaking up with hustle culture in whatever way it has shown up in your life. Perhaps that means creating firmer boundaries around work, refusing to do things for the sake of performance and replacing that with intention and service, or, if you find yourself hustling for survival, simply reminding yourself that *this is not your fault* and is not the life God intended for you. The journal prompts at the end of the chapter will help you break all of this down. I've got you.

However, as you are doing this inner healing work as the book goes on, I want you to begin considering the bigger picture. I want you to begin to think about what role you can play in working to dismantle this system that has done nothing but destroy us all from the moment it came into existence.

What part of this hustle culture machine do you want to devote yourself to working to demolish, and what would its demolition free you to focus on? Complete the journal prompts below so you can break up with hustle culture within yourself for good.

Actually, take a nap first.

You've done a lot already by completing this chapter. Hustle culture will tell you to keep going and not stop until everything is completed and you take an Instagram-worthy picture to prove it. So, in the spirit of divesting, do the opposite. Take a nap. Savor the journal prompts. Rest for a few days before you pick this book back up again if you need to. Take a slow walk with your family.

You have nothing to prove to anyone.

Your path is your own.

You are worthy.

Journal Prompts

1. Prior to reading this book, and more specifically this chapter, what was my understanding of capitalism, and how has it changed?

2. In what ways have I allowed hustle culture to become my idol, or even a god that I worship?

3. How have I justified hustle culture until now?

4. If my relationship with hustle culture is a privileged one (i.e., chasing success rather than hustling for survival), how can I use my privilege to reduce the need to hustle for those who have no choice?

5. How has hustle culture stripped me of my self-worth and caused me to believe in yet another way that I am not good enough?

6. What hustle culture lies about myself must I unlearn now?

7. How can I begin removing hustle culture from my life?

7

The Crisis We Refuse to See

It was a quiet afternoon. I was home alone. Reveling in my self-loathing thoughts.

I suck.

I hate myself.

No one wants me here.

I'm a screw-up.

I'm a mistake.

I hate myself.

This soundtrack of self-hatred played on repeat. I can't remember what triggered me that day. If I'm honest, I can't remember many of the finer details of the mental health struggles of my teenage years. I just remember the feelings. The feeling of isolation—as if the walls of my house were closing in on me. The feeling of stepping outside of my body—becoming so wrapped up in the intensity of uncontrollable anxiety that I could barely remember who or where I was.

Whenever I think back to that time, I just feel this . . . intenseness in my chest. That's how I can best explain it. This closed up, intense feeling in my chest that was accompanied by an immense need to either run away, hurt myself, or both.

Except that day was different. I'm not sure what it was . . . but that day, I wanted to end my life. My mother wasn't home. The timing was perfect. I felt like such an unworthy screw-up that I just knew there was no way she would miss me. I snuck upstairs to her room, fearful that somehow she would hear my loud steps from wherever she was at the time. I figured there had to be something in her medicine cabinet I could take that would end my life. Something . . . anything . . .

There was nothing. Not one thing I saw that would take me off this earth. Not finding the pills that day saved my life. That, and I chickened out. But I don't say that to minimize the seriousness of that situation. Saying that I "chickened out" almost makes it sound like a joke. Like I wasn't serious about wanting to end my life. But I was so serious. I was so tired of hating myself, of feeling like the biggest mistake to walk this earth. I was so tired of feeling like no matter how hard I pushed myself to be everything everyone required me to be, I wasn't good enough. I didn't want to feel like a burden anymore. I knew I was only here because my intellectually disabled biological mother accidentally got pregnant and didn't know it until it was too late for her to terminate the pregnancy. I knew I was never supposed to be here, I would never be good enough for those who were stuck taking care of me, and I was better off gone for good.

I wish my story was unique. Lord, do I wish my story was unique. I wish there weren't so many struggling humans on this earth who have thought to themselves, *Everything would be better if I wasn't here.* I wish there weren't so many of us who have not only thought those thoughts but have lost their battle with mental health as a result of those thoughts becoming just too much to bear. My heart aches for everyone who is fighting this battle right now. My heart mourns for everyone who has lost this battle. My heart is angry with the way we have created an entire society on the premise that the majority of us are inferior and that we must spend our entire lives "fixing" our inferiority and "earning" our worthiness.

My story wasn't unique among my peers in high school. Several of the girls I associated with had similar thoughts and feelings about harming themselves and ending their lives due to that same brutal belief that we weren't good enough. We connected in our collective despair, commiserating with one another as we felt we had no one else to turn to. I truly believe that we kept each other alive those years, and for that, I am grateful. But it shouldn't have ever had to get to that. No human, let alone a child, should ever have to feel like their presence isn't worthy on this earth. Yet suicidal ideation is only increasing among children and teens.[1] And sadly, it is children and teens whose mental health is often taken the least seriously and shown the least amount of empathy, especially within marginalized communities. Especially within the Black community.[2]

Growing up, any emotion I expressed that was negative, or in some way communicated that I was unhappy with something in my life for whatever reason, was often perceived as ungrateful and disrespectful. This is not at all uncommon, especially in Black families. When you consider the plight of the Black community and all we've had to—and continue to—endure, you're taught to just be grateful you have a roof over your head and food on the table because that is a feat in and of itself. But it's not just about gratitude. If it was, it would be so much easier to break this stigma. Since the beginning of the creation of racist ideas, Black people have existed in this world knowing that we are only viewed as inferior. While we most certainly don't see ourselves this way, we know that we must walk through a world that does, and that unless we are in the privacy of our own homes, we will always be viewed as inferior.

So much of what Black people do, whether knowingly or not, is in response to the trauma that comes with centuries of being viewed and treated as subhuman, begging for the white world to *finally realize* that we are just as good as they are. Because this is how we have been forced to walk through the world, we are extremely cautious about partaking in anything that will make us look like there is something wrong with us. We learned from the moment we were trafficked here in chains that our response to the never-ending racist terror could be nothing more than a stiff upper lip and a dependency on God for mere survival. Emotion was a sign of weakness and was never to be expressed. Emotion would just give the white men another reason to justify their inferior view of our bodies.

Yet it is that racist terror that causes the Black community to be 20 percent more likely to report serious psychological distress than white adults.[3] Though our existence alone subjects us to some of the greatest racist trauma to ever be experienced in Western society, we have believed that our response to that trauma, and any other hardship we endure, must be resilience. Asking for help means you're a failure as a person and cannot handle the challenges that "God will see you through." Because, how dare we ever allude to the white man that we might just be human after all? We can't. Society has taught us that we don't have the privilege of being human.

I write from the perspective of being a Black woman, so my personal stories and even historical viewpoint will always reflect that perspective. I never want to attempt to tell the story of another marginalized group when that is not a lived experience I can relate to. However, excluding the effects of white supremacy on the mental health of all marginalized communities also does a major disservice while communicating a misleading message that only Black people experience racist terror that is worth mentioning. Nothing could be further from the truth.

Indigenous peoples have experienced the deadliest, gravest, most brutal racial terror and cultural erasure from Western society, and as a result, experience the highest rates of depression among all marginalized groups.[4] The biracial community and the LGBTQIA+ community experience the highest rates of mental illness at 35.8 percent and 47.4 percent respectively, which shows a direct correlation to how, when you exist at the intersection of multiple marginalized identities in our white supremacist society, you also experience higher rates of racial and societal trauma, leading to higher rates of psychological distress.[5] These rates have only increased within the last few years as modern-day lynchings, anti-Asian hate crimes, LGBTQIA+ discrimination, and overall blatant racism are more visible than ever before, due to the ability to view viral videos of domestic terror and racist abuse on social media, retraumatizing us every time we unlock our iPhones.

Every single marginalized group is disproportionately affected by mental health issues compared to cishet white people due to related trauma alone; however, mental illness is on the rise among every person group in our society, regardless of race, gender, ability, or socioeconomic status.[6] And I don't think this is a surprise. The same system that was built to dehumanize and terrorize Black, Indigenous, People of Color has dehumanized and terrorized us all. We are all drowning. And as much as our society's leaders would love to chalk it up to the COVID-19 pandemic, the pandemic is not to blame. It has only exacerbated a problem that has been brewing since Western civilization seized perfectly content nations, selling the oppressive ideology of their civilization as "freedom" and "God's divine will."

There has been an increase of 664,000 adults who have reported having serious thoughts of suicide since 2011–2012. Currently, 19 percent of youth (ages twelve to seventeen) in the United States have reported experiencing major depression, and fewer than one in three youth will receive treatment for their depression.[7] And, as I mentioned, the pandemic has only exacerbated this already growing crisis. There has been such an increase in demand for mental health services since the pandemic started that therapists are forced to turn patients away, including children in grave distress.[8]

And, among every single mental health rate increase we have seen, the most alarming rates have been in children and youth. Our children are silently suffering, struggling with thoughts and acts of suicide at younger and younger ages. Of course, no one ever deserves to feel unworthy or unwanted, but especially not our babies. Just this past year, the U.S. Surgeon General declared the suicide rates amongst our youth to be an official epidemic.[9] The proof is in the pudding. Society has been failing us.

The Mental Health Warning Lights Have Been Flashing

You may be thinking, *Well, if society has failed us, why have poor mental health rates only been increasing within the past ten or fifteen years? If all of this is due to a system of white supremacy that was constructed hundreds of years ago, why are we just now seeing such a sharp rise in severe mental illness?* I'm glad you asked.

We have spent so much time focusing on the historical implications of white supremacy to help us understand just how this system has built upon itself to create the culture of white supremacy we live within today. We have focused on a few areas of society where white supremacy culture is most visible: within the school system, the beauty industry, and hustle culture. But we have *not* talked about how white supremacy culture, and the detrimental impacts of this culture, have not only gotten dramatically worse throughout history but exponentially worse in the current millennium.

The harder you fight an oppressive system, especially without attacking it at the root, the harder that system fights back. An oppressive system is only able to exist when there is something, or someone, to oppress. People cannot uphold their power if there is nothing to lord their power over, so the more that those subject to control *fight that power*, the more those in power will tighten their reins of control.

White supremacy was built to be a system of oppression. If it is not actively oppressing, it is not doing its job. Throughout history, we have fought to end specific systems of oppression (within the system as a whole) one by one, and one by one white supremacy has found a different way to regain control. We fought to end slavery, but white supremacy created the crime clause within the Thirteenth Amendment, and to this day forced labor is legal if you are considered to be a criminal.[10] We fought to end Jim Crow, and white supremacy retaliated with color-blind legal jargon purposefully intended to keep neighborhoods separate and keep Black people from having access to jobs, facilities, and other privileges white people had. We have fought to end modern-day lynchings and police brutality against Black bodies, yet the more we yell "Black Lives Matter," the more these killings occur.

We have fought for suffrage and women's equality, and to this day there are no laws that protect a woman's right to equal pay, a woman's right to guaranteed maternity leave, a woman's right to breastfeed or pump in public for her baby, a woman's right to make reproductive decisions, or even a woman's right to rest while she's on her period without risking her job. We have fought for the LGBTQIA+ community to legally marry whomever their heart desires, and though this right has only been in place since 2015, there are active discussions to overturn this victory.

We have fought, and fought, and fought, and begged, and prayed for mass shootings to end in this nation. Yet right in the middle of a sharp rise in mass shootings, some being racist domestic terrorist attacks, gun laws have been loosened instead of restricted, because the right to own guns was created to uphold white power over enslaved Black bodies, and any law that upholds power is always protected over laws that protect the lives of marginalized—and in turn, all—people. These are all systemic, more obvious examples of how white supremacy fights back against anything that tries to steal its power. Now let's look at the not-so-obvious cultural implications of white supremacy culture and how it is actively tearing away at our mental health the more we stand up to the harm this culture has caused us.

First, a quick reminder that the construction of white supremacy is based on the original belief that the cultural *interpretations* of Western Christianity were superior and thus should be the default societal and cultural practices of the nation. Those cultural interpretations include the beliefs that Christian Europeans were the standard of intellectualism, innovation, and elitism, and that this standard must be upheld always; that being God's "chosen" people justified genocide and brutality, causing generational psychological damage; that a woman's place was *only* in the home and submission both prevented women from escaping from abusive marriages and placed blame for that abuse on women; that children were to be controlled; and that only Christian men were allowed full access to all human and civil rights. Women, children, People of Color, LGBTQIA+ individuals, and disabled folks were inferior, were subhuman, and deserved rights be withheld from them.

Anyone who exists in a constant state of oppression will suffer mentally. Especially from oppression that is constructed systemically

163

and reinforced by culture. The only difference between then and now is the awareness of that psychological suffering. Up until recently, mental illness was only recognized in its most severe states, like schizophrenia or bipolar disorder. Anxiety, depression, and even general feelings of stress weren't recognized as a matter of mental health but as a matter of weakness, and were encouraged to be kept hidden. But silenced suffering does not equal a lack of suffering. It is just proof of the stronghold that oppression holds over those who are in bondage to it.

If you look at the patterns of history, you can see how almost every cultural change in our society is a desperate response to those most affected by white supremacy and the culture it was creating. First and foremost, the advancements of our society have just strengthened white supremacy as a whole, which just strengthened the effects of white supremacy culture throughout our lives. It's important to understand that this culture has only gained momentum since its inception, regardless of any attempts to fight its oppression. That gained momentum has increased psychological distress.

Historically, as that psychological distress increased and eventually brought people to their breaking point, drastic measures were taken to end the systems of oppression that were causing it in the first place. They may not have had the awareness we have now about exactly what mental health is. They may not have had the terminology or scientific studies to describe the anxiety, depression, and anger felt as a response to a society that was gaining oppressive momentum. But they obviously knew that something wasn't right, or they wouldn't have fought so hard to make changes.

Women wouldn't have stood up to how incredibly misogynistic and dehumanizing it was to be withheld from the workforce, to be denied suffrage, and to not have bodily autonomy if they hadn't felt some sort of psychological distress from living within such restrictive confines for generations. Over the years, we've seen women rejecting traditional gender roles, expressing more sexual freedom, and changing the ways they presented themselves to reflect that rejection of the normalized culture of patriarchy, misogyny, and the belief that there is only one right way to be a woman. I view these cultural statements as potential attempts to counteract the mental distress caused by the specific oppressive systems that kept women in a place of isolation, restriction, and control.

However, the backlash wasn't far behind, because white supremacy refuses to let go of power. So, the more women have fought for their equality, the more they have been silenced in other matters, such as sexual abuse, motherhood demands, and, most recently, reproductive healthcare.

The more women have fought for freedom, the heavier the burden they have had to carry as the standards of white supremacy culture, which are drenched in patriarchy, demand that women either find a way to behave exactly like white men or sit down and shut up. The more that women scream from the rooftops that the lack of support from our society for motherhood is crushing them, the more society restricts support for mothers, declaring that if mothers want to "compete for success in this world," they have to figure it out on their own. The more women fight, the stronger the backlash. The stronger the backlash, the more societal pressures and demands increase. The more societal pressures and demands increase, the higher the mental health crisis rate climbs.

Black Americans wouldn't have marched, refused to ride the bus, conducted sit-ins in public venues, and more if they held warm and fuzzy feelings about being racially terrorized and kept from societal advancement. And, in that fight, Black Americans rejected cultural white standards of beauty by embracing their natural hair, unapologetically expressing more of their Blackness in public, and standing against cultural assimilation. However, once again, the backlash wasn't far behind. We've already talked about the legal backlash, but culturally, Black people experience more intensified discrimination when we choose to reject assimilation and exist in the world in the fullness of our Blackness. And, while that's what most of us must do while facing the backlash of white supremacy culture, the mental toll can be debilitating.

The LGBTQIA+ community wouldn't have fought for their right to marry their partners if they didn't feel the immense pain of having to live in secret and never marry the love of their lives. During their fight, we saw the LGBTQIA+ community create the Pride movement, finally revealing to the world the truth about who they are and rejecting the heteronormative rules of white supremacy culture. And, as I'm sure you're picking up on the theme here, the more the LGBTQIA+ community rejects heteronormative standards, the more backlash they receive, such as novels featuring queer characters being banned from school libraries, a rise in anti-trans bills targeted toward trans youth, and so-called Don't Say Gay bills in some states that would prohibit teachers from having LGBTQIA+-centered conversations and instruction in their classrooms, if passed.[11]

America's workers would not have fought for nearly seventy-five years to establish a forty-hour workweek if they felt no physical or mental harm from the brutal working conditions and unfair labor practices. Now many are realizing that even the forty-hour workweek has begun to take its toll, as the growing demands of white supremacy and capitalism have forced so many into chronic burnout that keeps them from enjoying the products of their labor.

We have attempted, for centuries, to reject and fight against these individual systems of oppression, but we have yet to fight the umbrella system under which each of these systems dwells. The umbrella still stands. The foundation has not been shaken. The house of white supremacy has just continued to expand. Fighting each system has been like trying to knock down a room within a house that's still standing on solid ground. A little damage to that room might be done, but then the builders come in and repair the room, and make improvements to it, and to the house as a whole, to increase its effectiveness and longevity.

And with that remodeled house of oppression, the culture of white supremacy just becomes more brutal than it already was. The retaliation against women's rights has caused more women to experience debilitating depression and feelings of unworthiness as they are forced to "measure up" to the patriarchal standards that rule our world. The retaliation against Black, Indigenous, People of Color seeking expansion and protection of their rights has resulted in increased racialized terror, bolder expressions of racism on social media, and full-on bans of cultural and anti-racist education in schools and businesses, leading to BIPOC feeling more ostracized than ever before.[12]

The retaliation against the abusive culture of the workplace has not only led to an increase in demands of the labor force like limited bathroom breaks for warehouse workers[13] but also an increase in demands of our society's youth in school, believing that an increase in standards will push some sort of magical button in our children to make them more competitive against their peers across the globe.[14] Yet those increased demands have only been accompanied by a decrease in mental health support and programming for our children that will actually *improve* mental health; an increase in teachers who are progressively overworked, underpaid, and abused by the system; an increase in students being left behind in a system that was never built for their flourishing; an increase in bullying and isolation, leading to children not only ending their own lives but ending the lives of their peers, leaving children scared to go to the place that once made them feel at home; and so much more.

The present-day mental health crisis should not be a shock. The warning lights have been flashing since the first brick of the white supremacy foundation was laid. It has all led to this pinnacle moment. We are officially over capacity. We have been pushed past our limits. Our souls can't take it anymore, and they shouldn't have had to "take it" to begin with.

No more can we just tweet "thoughts and prayers" when another mass shooting happens, comment a bunch of heart emojis on the Instagram profile page of yet another person who loses their battle with mental health, or continue to act like we are okay as we swipe to that perfect filter on Instagram to put on a good show while feeling empty or heartbroken on the inside.

No longer can we stay silently complicit as white supremacy culture marches on just because something doesn't impact us as severely as it does others because of the positions of privilege we find ourselves in. No longer can we just try to make a few improvements within this abusive system, hoping that this time something will magically change, as if the repetitive nature of history has taught us nothing.

Your Most Important Battle

I continued to harm my body until my midtwenties. Not nearly as often as I did when I was in middle and high school. Just periodically. When the weight of the world and the crushing waves of unworthiness crashed over me with no escape in sight. I ran out of stamina . . . ran out of fight . . . ran out of the wherewithal to keep reaching toward standards and expectations I would just never be able to adhere to.

I hadn't become that successful career woman I was expected to become. No amount of hard work would change that. I had replaced those career standards with the perfectionist standards of mother-hood, and I was failing at those too—drowning in my inability to keep up with every demand of "biblical wifehood and motherhood." I had driven myself insane by falling for the belief that success only came when I did everything myself and never asked for help, since I still believed that asking for help meant admitting defeat. I still looked in the mirror and hated myself.

At every attempt to grasp for something I could control and some-thing I could succeed at, I unhealthily obsessed over my appearance, making sure that every nail was always painted and every hair was in place. I sacrificed much-needed sleep to go on 5:00 a.m. runs, never missing a morning, desperately seeking control and success by way of a "post-baby snatch-back." Whenever I made a mistake while trying to meet any of the demands of new motherhood, I still whispered, "You suck, Caroline. Get it together. You should be able to handle all of this. What is wrong with you?" just as my five-year-old, twelve-year-old, and seventeen-year-old self had done.

I never thought I would see the other side of that Caroline. I never thought I would see the day I no longer immediately thought of harming myself when the demands of life became too much to bear. I never thought I would see the day I no longer felt disgusted with who I was—someone unable to live up to the standards of society. I never thought I would be the person marveling at herself in the mirror, swaying my hips back and forth while I belt out Beyoncé's "Cozy" at the top of my lungs: "Comfortable in my skin, cozy with who I am." I never thought I would finally love the person staring back at me.

I love this for me. And I want this for you. You deserve this joy. You deserve to love yourself *big* and express that self-love without inhibition. And I know you will get there. It will be a battle. A lifelong battle. I fight my battle every day. I'm much further along than I've ever been, but dancing to "Cozy" in the mirror doesn't mean my battle is over. Far from it. The difference now is that I'm equipped with more knowledge and tools than I've ever had to be able to fight effectively and maintain my strength on those tough days that try to take me out. This book was designed to give you a few tools for your own battle.

If you take nothing else from this book, please understand just how detrimental the impact of our society has been on all of our mental health. Personally, I don't believe anyone is exempt from this impact. And I don't believe anyone is exempt from the need to heal from the trauma endured, regardless of how that looks for each of us. If you do nothing else, *fight for your mental health*. Fight for your healing. Go to therapy if you can. There are more affordable therapy options becoming available as the awareness around the importance of mental health becomes more normalized. However, if you can't afford a therapist right now, dedicate fifteen minutes a day to your healing through journaling, prayer, meditation, and reading more books to help you with your journey. Create the community for yourself that society has tried to take from you, even if that means your new bestie is someone you met on Instagram. Move your body, fuel your body, and treat your body with the utmost kindness. Set boundaries for yourself and uphold them without apology. Utilize the knowledge you now have about the truth behind society's demands to rewire how your brain perceives the world. I'll be giving you specific steps for this process in part 3, but for now, try to start identifying where your brain needs a bit of rewiring. Most importantly, trust yourself. Remember, *you* are the standard. You are worthy of your own trust.

The battle for your mental health may very well be the most important battle you fight for the rest of your life. There will be grief, anger, frustration, and even loneliness as you fight for your healing. And you will have to fight every day to remind yourself and live out the fact that you were created to be free. Fully free. Free in the way that Jesus intended for us to be free and *not* "free" in the way in which oppression disguises itself as freedom. Jesus freed us from the stain of sin, which I believe includes not only our own sin but *freedom from the stain of the sin of others*. We do not have to allow ourselves to be subjected to the brutality of an oppressive society that was created out of the sins of greed, pride, envy, and hatred of those who came before us. We do not have to chase ridiculous standards that were originally created in the bigoted name of racial and religious superiority just because they have now become normalized. Freedom was never meant to look like trying to earn our self-worth by chasing unattainable perfection. We have always been free from ever having to earn our self-worth or prove ourselves to anyone. All we're doing is reclaiming the freedom that has always been rightfully ours.

My number one hope is that this book helps you reclaim your freedom. But I would be remiss if I didn't emphasize the importance of taking your freedom and using it to demolish the system that stole your freedom in the first place. The entire system must be destroyed. Within yourself *and* the world. The house must be shattered, including its foundation. The machine must be annihilated and eradicated. The rotten tree must be uprooted and burned. It is not good enough to just spread this message to individuals and allow everyone to choose whether they want to believe they are free from white supremacy. Our debilitating mental health is the battle cry of our society begging us to *do something*. And that *something* is destroying white supremacy.

Jesus may give us a choice as to whether we want to follow him, but he does not give us a choice about dismantling systems of oppression.[15] Your choice in following Jesus should never have any bearing on whether you are subjected to oppression. Liberation from oppression is not reserved for those who follow Jesus. Jesus came to liberate *everyone*, whether or not they called him the Messiah. Humans should never be subjected to oppression and should have never *been* subjected to oppression, especially in the name of Jesus. That alone is the ultimate definition of hypocrisy, yet it is exactly what got us here in the first place. It is now time for us to destroy the system that those who came before us built in the name of the God they claimed to worship.

Not only is our soul, freedom, and humanity in our hands, but the soul, freedom, and humanity of every single person who has ever whispered to themselves, "I'll never be good enough. It would be better if I wasn't here," is also in our hands.

If that doesn't wake us up, I don't know what will.

Journal Prompts

1. Now that I understand the root of white supremacy culture and the lies I was conditioned to believe as true, how has white supremacy culture impacted my mental health? Can I make connections between my mental health struggles (like anxiety and depression) and systemic struggles that I wasn't aware of before?

2. What is something I have mistaken for normalized behavior that I now realize is a mental struggle that resulted from white supremacy culture?

3. What mental health support do I need as I journey through healing?

Part 3

Finding
Freedom

8

Stop Chasing

You're almost at the end of the book. Just a few more chapters to go. You've made it to the part where you break up with the chase **for** *clap* **good** *clap*. This is where the deep inner work you've been doing leads to your official breakup with white supremacy culture. This is the moment where you say, "Bye, Felicia. It's not me, it's *you*."

You've learned about what white supremacy is, where it came from, and how it led to the development of this tumultuous culture. You've begun to see the lies that white supremacy culture has brainwashed you into holding as doctrine. You've also learned about how society as a whole has reached its breaking point and how the only way we can put an end to this generational harm is to dismantle the entire system. You've done some inner work to uncover how white supremacy culture has kept you in bondage personally and how you may feel called or led to aid in the demolition of the system.

Now it's time to put it all into practice and discuss action steps for how you can strategically divest yourself from white supremacy culture and the lies of unworthiness it has sold you so you can officially create room for your freedom.

A few key points before we begin. First, breaking up with white supremacy culture, and most notably the *standards* of white supremacy culture, is not an excuse to never hold yourself accountable for anything. I feel like this goes without saying, but I want to make sure I'm communicating effectively. This is not an excuse to never admit when you've made a mistake or never own up to any wrongdoing. This is not an excuse to stop doing things with intention, purpose, or dignity. This is not an excuse to let responsibilities fall by the wayside and chalk it up to your new liberation journey. No, no, no.

Second, it's important for you to know that even though the principles are the same, how you choose to divest from white supremacy culture within your personal life may look different from the choices of someone else who is on the same journey. The application of these principles is personal to you and something only you can decide. You are not being graded. There are no standards here. You don't have to get it "right." It won't look perfect every day. There are *infinite* right ways to do it. The only "wrong" is anything that further perpetuates white supremacy, which may happen unintentionally as you get used to this new way of approaching life. That's okay. Remember to give yourself all the grace. You are choosing to walk through life in a new way after spending every moment before this one complying with white supremacy culture. Your instincts are that compliance. Choosing liberation will feel like rebellion—almost like you're doing something wrong. That's how you know you're on the right track.

Finally, breaking up with white supremacy culture also doesn't mean you can't ever set a goal, dream big, or have high aspirations. It doesn't mean you can't want to earn as many college degrees as your heart desires—it just means you don't *have to* earn degrees to prove yourself worthy. It doesn't mean you should feel guilty for either wanting to work toward a specific goal or for anything you've achieved in your life thus far—it just means your identity is not in your accomplishments. Goals, dreams, and successes, no matter how "big" or "small," do not define your worth, but they can be an integral part of what makes you *you*. That's not a bad thing. Having a drive or zeal for something, I believe, is how God whispers his plan to use us in this mighty world he has created—each of us doing our part with every action-filled *and* rest-filled step we take. Breaking up with white supremacy culture just means replacing the deep-seated fear it has ingrained in us that we are unworthy unless we achieve, accomplish, or perform to white supremacy's standard with *knowing* that no amount of achievement, or lack thereof, will ever change our value as human beings. It is replacing the *need to achieve* by keeping up with the demands with the *desire to serve* with intention and grace, never putting our humanity on the back burner while doing so.

Think back to the list of characteristics we talked about in chapter 3. Instead of letting those characteristics lead us into a life of striving and seeking an unattainable standard, let's replace them with characteristics that open us up to a more holistic and inclusive way of viewing ourselves and others, outside of the weight of white supremacy culture.

We replace perfection with *growth*.

We replace binary thinking with *embracing nuance*.

We replace the pressure to perform with the *joy of living*.

We replace chasing something we aren't with *adoring who we are*.

We replace power grabbing with *redistribution and equity*.

We replace our obsession with quantity with an obsession with *quality*.

We replace individualism with *community*.

We replace false objectivity with *embracing emotion and empathy*.

And, most importantly, we reject the idea that white, Eurocentric *anything* is the standard. We replace the idea that there is one perfect standard with the truth that there is no one standard. We all get to be the standard. Every culture, every religion, every gender, every ethnicity, every identity, and every worldview *gets to be the standard*.

Break Up with the Standard

So, that is the first step. In every way that white supremacy culture has tried to condition you into accepting that whiteness and Eurocentrism are the standard, break up with it.

Where this belief shows up in your life may shock you. It goes much further than what we were able to cover in this book. We discussed the major, more obvious standards of whiteness most of us can see from any angle of society; however, don't forget you have a personal perspective—a worldview influencing your mindset that only *you* can identify with. Perhaps you were taught something specific in primary school about a certain way to speak, and that the "wrong" way to speak was associated with certain ethnic or racial groups that were inferior. Perhaps you were taught that certain religious practices were equivalent to moral superiority because they were Eurocentric in nature, and you need to reevaluate your convictions. Perhaps you believe there is only one way to measure intelligence, and now you're realizing just how steeped in white supremacy your measuring stick is.

As you reflect and reevaluate your life, you're going to begin to have some *aha* moments—moments you realize a truth you held to was just another lie of white supremacy that you must now divest from. A big one for me was speaking. I was raised that there was a certain way to speak English, and if I engaged in speaking any African American Vernacular English (AAVE), I would come across as unintelligent—and those who did regularly speak AAVE *were* unintelligent. I spent the entirety of my primary years learning to "speak in a white voice" and reject any type of speech that reflected the cultural expression of Blackness that came more naturally to me. Not only was this internalized anti-Blackness that I needed to rid myself of, but it is also a common belief the majority of the population holds without shame because, once again, our conditioning is such that whiteness is the standard. However, this is what I would call a more subtle belief . . . one that you won't realize you have until you do the work to free yourself from white supremacy.

Another way I was idolizing whiteness without realizing it was in my relationship with God. In my early twenties, I began attending a church that was not predominantly Black for the first time. After growing up in the Black church, I'd never listened to any worship music that wasn't gospel, never heard a white person preaching, and never attended a church that didn't have full-on choir robes and foot-stomping as a norm. Yet when I encountered a predominantly white space and listened to Hillsong for the first time, I immediately internalized that style of worship as superior to what I had grown up with. Because it was white.

My internal conditioning of white supremacy was so embedded into my brain waves that I immediately threw one of the cornerstones of Black culture I had grown up with out the window just because I saw white people worship a different way and instantly believed their way was better. No other explanation except the fact that they were white. I justified it with the fact that white Christian worship felt like a rock concert and seemed to be deeper and more

"Spirit-filled" than Black worship. I made up any little rationalization I could as to why I thought white worship was superior.

I was brainwashed. I proudly stated that I would never go back to the Black church again. I took everything I learned from my new white evangelical church at face value and never questioned it. I just *knew* I was following Jesus "correctly" this time because I had found a church that was *upholding the standard.*

This particular realization of my brainwashing and complicity with white supremacy was probably the most heartbreaking one I've had on this journey. I spent ten years building a foundation of faith on the premise that whiteness was superior to Blackness. I worshiped with and took spiritual correction from pastors who viewed me as inferior but knew exactly how to cover up their racism with the perfect smile. I willingly allowed this conditioning to implant anti-Black rhetoric into my spirit and influence me into erasing my Blackness in exchange for "holiness."

The moment I realized what had been happening was the biggest *aha* moment in my divesting journey—and let me tell you, it's a moment that nearly took me out. It brought about unexpected grief, anger, disappointment, and even the revelation of trauma. It made me realize I had much more healing to do than I imagined when I first began this journey.

You will have similar moments that make you feel like the wind has been knocked out of you, where you realize something you put your wholehearted identity into has been a harmful, toxic lie all along. You will have moments of all-consuming grief and anger that you weren't expecting.

I never said this journey would be an easy one. The most liberating ones never are. But let God do this work in you. Let him reveal to you the deepest places of bondage he's been waiting to deliver you from.

Action Steps for Your Breakup

1. Identify the Standards You Have Normalized

I'm going to give it to you straight: this will probably be the longest, most emotional, and most exhaustive part of your process. But it will also be the most liberating. Nothing is more liberating than learning the truth.

(*This is exactly why the powers that be work so hard to keep the truth from us in school, in the media, and in politics, while convincing us that their narrative is the truth. Did I just give you a revelation?*)

Take heart, though, my friend. You are prepared for this part. You have learned what you need to know to identify where white supremacy has snuck its indoctrination into your life. Now you just need to tune in to yourself, your past, your upbringing, your surroundings, and your spirit to pinpoint the damage it has done.

I recommend taking a journal with you everywhere you go for the next few weeks. As you go through the intricacies of your day, whether they be the most mundane moments or monumental circumstances, lean into them delicately. Make note of when the pace of your breath intensifies because you're experiencing pressure. What event is causing that pressure? Why? Make note of the thoughts you have toward your circumstances and what perspective is shaping those thoughts.

Make note of your approach toward people when you're out in public and be honest with yourself. Do you tend to feel nervous or shy away from people? Do you immediately make judgments about people based on appearance? Do you try to make conversation with every person you interact with? Observe your thoughts and behaviors and make graceful notes about them without bias.

Make note of what you tell yourself when you look in the mirror. Are your first thoughts self-deprecating? Are you quick to point out all of your flaws and scramble to find the concealer? What emotions rise in your chest when you stop and stare at your body? Have you ever sat with those emotions?

Make note of the internal dialogue you carry when you feel like your back is up against the wall and your anxiety is rising. How do you speak to yourself? Do you punish yourself for your struggles, or do you handle yourself with care? Do you try to overcompensate for the anxiety by seeking control elsewhere? Or do you try to bury the anxiety and pretend it doesn't exist? Do you practice coping techniques, avoidant techniques, or sabotaging techniques? This is the time to be honest with yourself. You're not holding anything against yourself or judging yourself. You're just observing and documenting. The only "wrong" answers are dishonest ones.

Document your findings as close to the moment as possible. I know we all lead busy lives that don't necessarily cater to round-the-clock journaling, but you can take a few extra moments in your car before you head into the house, make a note on your phone when you're on the go, or journal with your coffee every morning before you scroll Instagram. Write your reflections while you are at the soccer game, on the subway, or right before you start folding that load of laundry. Ignore your handwriting. Don't try to form complete sentences. Just get your realizations out of your brain onto that paper.

After two or three weeks have passed, make a date with yourself to analyze the results of your journaling. Read everything you wrote and highlight any themes you notice. This is when you'll be able to pinpoint the detrimental standards you are holding yourself to and identify themes throughout. If you can, try to write down one or two standards that may be driving the behaviors, emotions, and thought patterns you observed. I recommend making a little chart in your journal that has four columns. The first section is your observed behavior. Rewrite your documented behaviors in a list format in the first column. In the second column, write the corresponding standard(s) you can identify for each behavior/thought pattern. The remaining two columns will be utilized in the next steps of this process.

2. Trace the Root of Each Standard

This is where you take the education you have received in this book, as well as any other books and articles you've read to dive deeper into these topics, and trace the specific white supremacy cultural roots of the standards you are holding yourself to. Is the standard you hold your body to rooted in the racist origins of fatphobia or colorism? Is the standard you hold your mind to rooted in the racist origins of how we measure scholastic achievement? Is the standard you hold your productivity to rooted in the power-hoarding, capitalist mindset that you're only as valuable as what you produce and that rest is only for lazy, unemployed people living off the welfare system? For each standard you've identified, try to identify a corresponding characteristic of white supremacy culture that you think may be the root of that standard. You may identify more than one, which is perfectly fine. In fact, it's encouraged. Write each characteristic in the third column of your chart so that it aligns with the corresponding standard and observed behavior in the first two columns.

If you're having a hard time identifying the root of the standard but have identified the standard itself, it may be that this particular root is not as obvious or wasn't covered in this book. For example, professionalism. We haven't covered that as much, but the idea of professionalism is another tenet of white supremacy culture, rooted in the racist idea that the attire of rich white men is the pinnacle representation of elitism and respectability. Thus, in order to demonstrate you are qualified to do work in a "skilled, white-collar industry," you must present yourself in a "professional manner," both physically (via attire) and intellectually (via speech/diction, educational credentials, and other protocol) to prove you deserve to work in a so-called higher-level position.

The truth is that most of the things we do in the name of professionalism don't have anything to do with one's qualifications to do a particular job. A thousand-dollar well-tailored suit doesn't make you more competent or eligible for a higher salary, and requiring these fabricated rules only serves the purpose of intentionally withholding opportunity from certain demographics who are already at a disadvantage when it comes to obtaining what "professionalism" requires. Recognizing the root of this idea of professionalism doesn't mean you must throw away all desire to dress in a manner that makes you feel esteemed in the work you do. It just means that you recognize your choice to dress a certain way doesn't place you above someone who doesn't dress like that. It also means that if you do choose to alter how you dress or present yourself in the workplace, you have the freedom to do so.

Essentially, you should be in an environment where you can relax, bring joy back to the simple things in your life, like how you express yourself, and leave the pressure to perform at the door. However, the focus right now isn't your response to the standard itself. That's the next step. I just know that if you're anything like me, you may think about multiple things at once and begin to get ahead of yourself, so I just want you to keep these things in mind as each revelation comes to you.

So, for each standard, write down where in white supremacy culture that standard originates from so you can speak directly to the lies, unlearn the racist/sexist/patriarchal biases, and detach yourself from the idol you have created of them. This is how you are uprooting the rotten tree. It feels hard, but a good hard, doesn't it?

3. Part Ways with the Standard

This is the moment. I know you're ready. You are going to break up with every single standard to which you have held yourself and, by default, others. You are officially declaring that white supremacy no longer has a hold on you.

In the fourth column, next to where you traced the root of the standard you held yourself to, write what *mindset* you will replace your former standard with. But you are not replacing a standard with another standard. I repeat: you are *not* replacing a standard with another standard. You are replacing a standard with *a renewed mindset*.

To continue with the professionalism example, you would replace the standard of professionalism you have held yourself to with the mindset that how you dress or speak is not a worthiness qualifier for you or anyone else. If you are replacing a standard from beauty culture, you might replace that with the mindset that there are no physical features that are more beautiful than other features. Make this specific to you by listing out particular physical attributes you have held on a pedestal.

Personally, hyperpigmentation on my face has been a big hurdle for me—believing that darker marks from acne and scars somehow make me ugly, especially since my skin is already dark. And while it's okay for me to want to use skincare to fade my dark marks, my choices should not be based on the premise that dark marks make me less beautiful. A mindset reframe would be that I want to care for my skin, as it is an organ that serves my body, but no matter what state my skin is in, it is beautiful and does not need to be covered up to make me appear more attractive.

Whatever your mindset shifts are, write them down in the fourth column. Take your time with this, and take breaks as needed. This is a mentally exhausting undertaking, and if you're feeling drained, it's okay. You're doing so much good, deep, hard work that most people don't even want to attempt to do. (Believe me, the fact that you even picked up this book after looking at the title means everything. Most people would've seen the words *white supremacy* on the cover and put it right back down.) Remember that the most freeing work is also the toughest, grittiest work—and the most worthwhile.

4. Make a Game Plan and Take Action Steps

Your renewed mindset is nothing without a game plan, which is exactly *how* you will put your renewed mindset into action. It is also how you will fight against the lies of white supremacy that will try to creep back into your mind. Your game plan doesn't have to be complex. I encourage you to keep it simple. Nothing is ever doable when it's complicated.

Let's stick with the standards we've been using as examples thus far, professionalism and beauty. We'll also talk a bit about perfectionism, which is something many of us struggle with, myself included.

If you've realized professionalism is a big one for you, and you've written down your renewed mindset, a simple game plan might be to begin varying your work wardrobe in a way you may have been apprehensive to do before now. A wardrobe can also include creative or natural expressions of hair, cosmetics, or anything else potentially ridiculed in the name of professionalism. How much action you want to take is up to you. You may want to go total activist style and challenge a dress code at work that you know is not serving anyone, or you could just wear some earrings you thought you couldn't because of how they stand out. You could also choose to do nothing, knowing that your choice to continue adhering to the perceived characteristics of professionalism is now your *personal choice*, not the pressure of the standard, as long as you know that your mindset behind your choice has changed.

A game plan for beauty standards may include an alteration to your makeup routine or choosing beauty styles you would normally shy away from because you didn't think your body was "good enough" to enjoy them. For me, it was a commitment to wearing less makeup, or none at all, and spending a few minutes each morning admiring myself in the mirror. I've since fallen in love with the marks on my face while having grace for the acne that loves to appear each month. It's not easy, as my default is self-ridicule, but with a dedicated mindset reframe, I just remind myself that my acne is a representation of my female hormones hard at work, especially as I've been putting in additional effort to heal hormonal imbalances caused by my years of disordered eating.

Now to address perfectionism—one of the main ways white supremacy culture has brainwashed us into believing we will earn our worthiness. How do you break up with perfectionism in a world that continues to demand it? I know it feels impossible. And it will require rebellion, boundaries, and continued mindset reminders as the world pushes against you.

Your game plan against perfectionism may include a commitment to believing "done" is better than perfect. It may include a commitment to saying no more often than you've ever allowed yourself to, because you know that another yes will lead to burnout. It may include an obligation to yourself to choose rest as an act of resistance anytime you feel the urge to perform beyond what is needed at the present moment. Commit to something simple and doable, yet transformative for you.

These are just a few examples, and none of them may relate to your specific findings, standards, and identified root characteristics of white supremacy culture. These examples are simply here to help you see the progression of the process and give you some ideas of how to approach your own journey. However, it is *your* journey.

187

Again, there are no wrong answers except dishonest ones. Trust yourself, don't overthink it, and take your time.

Living Out Your Liberation

Here's what they don't tell you about liberation—it is a daily *commitment*. It is not a one-time change of mindset and then you go merrily on your way. It is not a commitment to read a few books and think you learned something, but then fall back into old ways *without* recommitting anytime that slip happens. Liberation is a choice you make every day to live actively in a world that puts forth every effort to keep you in bondage.

You *can* do this. You *will* do this.

Your next steps in this journey include taking your personal liberation and committing to a lifetime of working toward liberating the world.

Before you turn the page, I recommend another pause. Finish your work here before you move on. I know it's tempting to hop on to the next thing, but that's just another lie of white supremacy that you need to reject. So take your pause, and then move through your work with intention and at a pace that is committed—yet your own.

Inhale: *I will commit to this journey because I deserve to be free.*

Exhale: *My journey is my own.*

Journal Prompts

1. Identify the standards you have normalized.
2. Trace the root of each standard.
3. Part ways with the standard and shift your mindset.
4. Make a game plan.
5. Take action steps.

9

Breaking the Cycle

"When I grow up, I'm going to be a mom! I'm going to take care of my kids—which will be *three*, by the way—and clean my house and be a writer!" my older daughter exclaims to me.

I look at her with admiration and pride, in awe of how big and limitless her dreams are. "What else?" I ask.

She proceeds to tell me all the other things she can't wait to do when she's a grown-up. Her career aspirations change daily. Sometimes she wants to be a writer like her mother, sometimes she wants to be a scientist like Ada Twist, and sometimes she wants to be a doctor just like Doc McStuffins. She often tells me she wants to be all three and just rotate between jobs while also heading off to space, building houses, and dancing on a big stage just like Misty Copeland. The one constant is that she is always a mother in her dreams. A mother with three children (her way of asking for a baby brother or sister) who homeschools her children just like she's homeschooled, who cleans the house just like her mother cleans the house, and who makes scones just like her mother makes scones.

My response never changes. "You can do it all, sis. You can do anything you want to."

(Note: I don't add "if you just work hard enough," or ask her what she wants to be, because that would just be continuing the vicious cycle of white supremacy. Right now, my goal is to instill a firm foundation of confidence in my daughters so that, as they mature and discover the realities of society, especially as Black girls, their belief in themselves is rock solid.)

My heart melts every time she lets me into her dream world. Not because she wants to be a mother and do things just like I do them, and certainly not because of what her idea of motherhood is. My heart melts because she sees *something* in me that she wants to aspire to, and she trusts me enough to pour her heart out to me. I don't take that lightly. Every time we have this conversation, I make sure to remind her that being a mom—if that's what she chooses— will only be a part of her, not her entire identity. I'm also honest with her about my own struggles so that she can see her mother is a human being who battles daily with the delicate balancing act of motherhood and person-with-big-dreams-hood. I don't want her to look at me and create a fantasy that she later realizes isn't filled with as many sparkles as she imagined. I want her to know firsthand the challenges she will face so that she is equipped for them while keeping her eyes on the prize and her feet firmly planted in her foundation of Black Girl Magic confidence. (I should note that all of this goes for both of my daughters, but my three-year-old isn't exactly having these conversations with me juuuust yet.)

It amazes me that my older daughter, just five years old, has already taken the most significant details of her life to put together a picture in her mind of what the future is supposed to look like. This is her worldview. She sees a mother who is home during the day and a father who works during the day, so she thinks this is what mothers and fathers do. She sees a mother who homeschools her children, so she thinks she should homeschool her children too. She sees a mother who is a writer, so she's taken her love of comic books and decided that she will write comic books when she grows up. She sees a mother who bakes homemade pastries and granola, so she wants to bake homemade pastries and granola. She sees a dad who can throw down on the grill, so she wants her future husband to do the same.

Most importantly, she envisions what *kind* of mother she wants to be and *how* she will care for and love her children. She practices her future role on her doll babies, reciting various parenting scenarios that I make sure to pay close attention to, because I know her role-playing is indicative of what's going on in her five-year-old brain. I know her playing is a way for her to communicate to me how she's processing everything she has gone through in her life thus far and is a reflection of how she's perceiving it all. I listen for what words and phrases she chooses to parent her dolls with and take note of how she handles it when her dolls "misbehave" or have a conflict with one another (yes, dolls fight over toys too). I listen for how she shows her dolls affection and what activities they do together, and if I can interpret anything about what my daughter may be feeling or needing that she may not have the words to communicate with me.

On the outside, it may seem like she wants to be just like me, and that everything she has experienced as my daughter has been nearly perfect, but I know there are things she has already vowed to do differently when she becomes a mother. Her parents are flawed humans who are just now realizing the depths of their trauma and just how much that trauma has unintentionally seeped into their parenting.

And while it's natural for children to disagree with choices their parents make, because boundaries are never fun when you're a kid, there's a difference between frustration with boundaries and passing our trauma along to our children because of our brokenness. It doesn't take children long to realize when something they've experienced, or have been on the receiving end of, *isn't quite right* and to begin dreaming of all the things they will say and do differently when it's their turn to raise children.

Children just *know*. I knew. I used to fantasize about all of the changes that I, too, would make when I became a mother. I fantasized about how I would react to my children's challenges, emotions, and other human moments that I felt I needed to suppress as a child. I fantasized about how often I would say the words "I love you," and how I would give copious hugs and kisses without my children having to silently yearn for them. I imagined the words I would say to correct my children's behavior without making them feel less valuable as human beings. I remember saying that I would never speak ill of my children to my adult friends, especially if my children were in earshot. I remember vowing to myself that I would never, ever do or say anything that would make my children feel like they were a burden, were unwanted, or had to earn my love.

When I finally became a mother, I remembered those vows I made to myself in my early childhood years. I figured it would be a piece of cake to honor them. I knew what to do and what not to do, what to say and what not to say. I was ready to break those generational cycles, and I knew that as soon as I held my baby in my arms, those chains would immediately fall off.

I was in for a rude awakening.

As soon as my baby learned how to talk and began to come into her personality, complete with opinions and behaviors that were almost always a contradiction of what I believed to be "right" or "acceptable," almost every single thing I had vowed not to do, I did. When I felt challenged, I yelled instead of getting on her level.

I began to see her as an inconvenience rather than a tiny human who was just struggling with her rapidly developing brain and big emotions. I began to resent those emotions, feeling as though they were too much for me to handle, instead of creating a safe place for her emotions to land. The more she pleaded for my attention, the more I withdrew, feeling frustrated that one tiny human could need so much from me. And when my withdrawal caused bigger emotional outbursts, I accused her of manipulation instead of owning up to the fact that she was responding to my unwillingness to meet her needs.

Every single time I broke those vows, it was as if I was having an out-of-body experience—similar to how I felt when I was deep in the throes of depression as a teenager. I wasn't myself. Something deep within the pit of my soul that I didn't even know existed had taken over me. And as soon as the damage was done, I snapped back to reality to find my precious girl staring back at me with immense sadness in her eyes. She just needed me to see her—to validate her emotions and create a space for her to let go without ever fearing that she wasn't enough, was too much, had to earn my love, or was unwanted. She needed exactly what I'd needed twenty-seven years prior when my little body was confused by the world around me and the needs I couldn't communicate had bubbled up inside of me, nearly bursting my seams.

Instead, I met her with exactly what I vowed to never do, exactly what I knew would mark the beginning of her wandering through life feeling as though her very existence was a mistake. Why? Why had I done that? And why, every single time I re-vowed to never do it again, did I *keep doing it*?

Because my trauma wasn't healed. Because I *wasn't healed*. I had never actually mended the wounds white supremacy had caused me—from the very way I was brought into this world, to my childhood difficulties, to my current adult battle with still feeling unworthy.

How could I raise a child to believe *she* was worthy if I still didn't believe *I* was worthy?

How could I make space for my child's emotions if I couldn't make space for my own because I still believed emotions were an inconvenience that demonstrated ungratefulness and weakness?

How could I pour endless amounts of love into my child if I had spent my entire life only pouring an endless amount of hate into myself?

I couldn't. It was impossible. Broken humans cannot heal other humans. And while I didn't need to heal my daughter per se, as the trials of the world had yet to reach her, I did need to do my part to help keep her whole, to serve as the foundation of how she views herself when she looks in the mirror.

It is only when I recognized that trauma was the culprit—and that the lies of white supremacy were the igniters of the trauma—that I was finally able to break the cycle I'd found myself in. Thankfully, even before breaking that cycle, I had enough awareness to realize that something was off and that those moments were not indicative of the parent I wanted to be. That awareness allowed me to repair the damage I caused by humbly apologizing to my daughter whenever I mishandled a situation and asking for her permission to try again. As I sought guidance from God, and he led me to the revelations that eventually brought me to write this book, I used the time in the interim to teach my daughter just how flawed we are as humans and what to do when our flaws get the best of us. All hope was not lost, but I also knew that this could not continue. I knew something had to be done to break both cycles—the cycle I found myself in with my daughter and the cycle I was carrying from previous generations into the next one.

The Weight of Generational Trauma

No one is immune to generational trauma. And no, I'm not just talking to the parents who are reading this book. We are *all* carriers of generational trauma, which is trauma passed down to subsequent generations from someone who directly experienced a traumatic incident.[1] Just vowing to "do things differently" is not enough. When we aren't in a state of feeling threatened, stressed, or in need of a fight-or-flight response, it's easy to say that we'll never allow something to happen that we know is harmful. The majority of us don't intend to cause the harm we perpetuate. It happens because we have issues within ourselves—whether they be unresolved traumas, unmet needs, or even harmful fallacies we believe—that rise to the surface as soon as something sets us off.

Every single one of us, as well as society as a whole, is the product of generational trauma that has not only been passed down but intensified with each generation. You could have had a childhood filled with rainbows and butterflies and still have generational trauma just by nature of the unknowingly toxic societal norms that haven't been challenged until now. You could have had a family that was quite aware of those toxic norms and did their best to teach you otherwise but still have been impacted by the generational trauma of society at large by way of the messaging received in school and through the media. You may exist in a marginalized body, and thus carry the weight of the trauma that marginalization has caused your community for generations. Or you could have witnessed deeply personal trauma beyond the scope of what I've talked about here and find yourself carrying the burden of your family's story and legacy on your shoulders, all while trying to heal from the pain you endured.

Whatever corner you find yourself in, you must acknowledge the very real wounds yearning to be healed. They aren't wounds you caused. They aren't your fault. You may even feel resistance to healing them because *you shouldn't have to be the one to carry this burden.* But if you don't, not only will you never be free but you will pass on those wounds—with even more salt added to them as they continue to fester—to the next generation of tiny humans who have done nothing to deserve such pain. Just as you didn't deserve to receive the wounds from generations prior, the next generation does not deserve to receive those wounds from you because you refuse to heal.

In the previous chapter, you took specific action steps to break up with white supremacy culture. So vital. However, this removal is not equivalent to healing from the wounds it has caused—both generationally passed down and freshly inflicted by white supremacy culture today. To break the cycle right now, healing must be your priority.

The hard part is that you will be healing for the rest of your life. You will not reach full healing on this side of heaven. And because we live in a culture of instant gratification and the need for measurable results, you will probably feel some resistance on this journey. You may feel impatient. You may feel like a failure, or like you "should have" overcome all of this "by now." You may have an overwhelming desire to give up and slip back into what feels comfortable. Trauma loves to trick us into believing that it is comfortable and safe. That's how it gets you to stay there—relying on it as a dwelling place so that you fear breaking free.

Do not confuse comfort with being stuck. I repeat: do not confuse comfort with being stuck.

Heal Like Your Life Depends on It, Because It Does

I wish I could tell you exactly how to heal, but I can't do that. All I can do is be a tool in your toolbelt, a cheerleader in your corner, and a safe space to land whenever you need it during your journey. This book can be the place where you remind yourself of what's a lie, what's true, why you're doing this, and what's at stake. This book can be the safe place you turn to when you feel inundated by an inescapable culture that feels like it may never progress. Re-read chapters as your soul needs you to, reminding yourself that every corner of society you face every day that continues to yell, "YOU ARE UNWORTHY!" is nothing but a culture constructed by people who felt so unworthy themselves that hoarding power by violently slaughtering and enslaving those they perceived to be beneath them was the only way they knew how to fabricate their false righteousness.

As much as I have learned, and as much work as I have done, my healing journey is just beginning. Healing will take a lifetime of therapy—digging into dark places that I'm not yet even aware exist. Healing will take a lifetime of shedding—shedding the layers of trauma, self-hatred, and lies that have been built like an exoskeleton around my soul. As much as I wish I could take an imaginary sledgehammer and pound through that thing so that I can reveal the real me I've yet to meet, I know it doesn't work that way. The shedding will be a slow, sometimes painful process that will only happen if I awaken each day with full commitment to doing the work. Not in a perfectionist way, but in a *my entire being depends on this* way. And in a *my children don't deserve my trauma* way.

Healing will look like **rest**. So much rest. Rest is work, and rest is resistance. Your overloaded, burdened soul cannot heal without long-overdue rest, just like our physical bodies can only heal when we are at rest. And because our society wants to deny you rest at every corner, you will have to demand it. You will even have to force it sometimes. You have to take back the rest that rightfully belongs to you, no shame or guilt attached.

Healing will look like **confrontation**. Again, you must confront the wounds that have been festering for generations as well as the wounds that are fresh from last week. Confrontation is not pretty. Confrontation is often ugly, fiery, and vulnerable. Confrontation forces you to see yourself. Not just look at yourself, but *see* yourself. You will have to see yourself as a child and face the scary feelings your survival has forced you to bury. You will have to see yourself right now—intricately looking at how society's harm has shaped the person staring back at you in the mirror. And you will have to see yourself healed, because if you don't, you'll begin to think the journey isn't worth it anymore. You have to force yourself to envision the healed version of yourself without reserve.

And healing will look like **forgiving**. Perhaps the hardest part is that healing cannot happen without forgiveness. It looks like not only forgiving those who have contributed directly to your pain but also forgiving those who caused the pain in those who caused you pain. It looks, perhaps oddly, like forgiving society for all of the harm it has caused for generations—not because society deserves it but because holding on to anger that keeps you stuck in the loop of reliving your trauma does nothing but prevent your progress. However, since our white supremacist society is still going strong, don't become too detached through that forgiveness. Keep the righteous anger that drives you to take action toward society's demolition, not stopping until it is finished.

Most importantly, healing looks like forgiving *yourself*. You've done nothing wrong, but you've still carried shame and guilt that weren't yours to carry. You deserve forgiveness for that. You *need* forgiveness for that.

There is no right or wrong first step to take in your healing. There is no right or wrong resource to use. This is your journey. Your path. Your body. Your mind. Your spirit. You have to decide what is right for you.

I can, however, tell you to take your time. I can tell you that you must be committed. I can tell you that it's okay to need help. I can *encourage* you to seek help. I have provided resources, journaling prompts, information, and support to help you wherever your healing path takes you. And, of course, I have helped you start breaking up with white supremacy culture and working toward the demolition of the entire system.

It's a huge undertaking, I know. You are being tasked with dismantling white supremacy culture in your daily life while healing from the wounds it has caused you so that you don't unintentionally pass those wounds along to the next generation. This is groundbreaking, world-changing work. It is also grueling, taxing, and exhausting work. But I believe we were born for such a time as this. I believe we were called to *this* generation for *this* very moment. The pain we've endured can spur us on to make the changes every human has been internally pleading for since the moment white supremacy became the dominant system of oppression in our world.

It's time to get started. You've broken up with white supremacy culture, and now it's time to commit to healing. Take a deep breath—and take it one step at a time. At the end of your journal prompts is space to write out your commitment to healing statement as well as action steps you plan to take to carry out that commitment, whether that's seeking therapy, writing a letter to your past self or people who have hurt you, or finding a support group. I've provided brainstorming space as well for you to just get the ideas flowing. Give yourself a first step you can take without feeling overwhelmed. Nothing is final, as healing is fluid. I invite you to come back to this space or write in a separate journal that makes it easier to come back to so that you can make any changes necessary as your journey flows with you.

Remember, there are no right or wrong answers. You have nothing to prove. You're already enough.

But most importantly, you deserve to heal. You deserve freedom.

Journal Prompts

1. What generational wounds do I need to commit to healing from?

2. What realizations about generational trauma have I made since reading this book? How has generational trauma affected me in ways I haven't realized until now?

3. What other traumas (not necessarily generational) do I need to heal from? How has this trauma affected my well-being and daily living?

4. My commitment to healing

    a. My brainstorming of thoughts:

    _____

    _____

    _____

    _____

    _____

    _____

    _____

b. My commitment to healing statement:

_____

_____

_____

_____

_____

_____

c. My healing action steps:

_____

_____

_____

_____

_____

_____

10

We'll All Be Free

I want to start this chapter with a beautiful, inspiring story.

You know how when you get to the end of a book, you're excited because you've reached the happily ever after? You expect the last chapter to give you rainbows and butterflies and to tie a nice bow around everything you've read thus far. You expect the anecdote of the last chapter to be the uplifting one. The powerful one. The hopeful one.

I want that for us too. So I sit and stare at the blank page, trying to force my brain to come up with something. I stare and I stare, and then I stare some more. I pray, as I have before every chapter, and ask God to give me an empowering story that would leave you skipping off into the sunset with nothing but motivation and excitement for the newly liberated life that awaits you.

Yet the more I try to force myself to think of that magical story, the more I just keep visualizing George Floyd fighting for his life on the pavement of Chicago Avenue in my hometown of Minneapolis. Tears well in my eyes. I can still so clearly hear his cries for his mama as he took his last breaths. It's been two years since his lynching, and the pain from that day has only intensified, especially since the "racial reckoning" that followed was so short-lived that all we had to do was blink before the people who vowed to fight against white supremacy once and for all went back to business as usual.

My mind then jumps to the video of Ahmaud Arbery being lynched just for being a Black man who dared to jog through a white neighborhood. This lynching incited a paralyzing fear throughout the Black community of going for an innocent jog—something that no human should ever have to fear. Yes, his murderers were convicted in a historic trial, which is proof of progress, but it doesn't change the fact that the lynching happened—that lynchings are *still* happening. That Black, Indigenous, People of Color cannot freely exist in the society they are supposed to call home without being subjected to racial trauma every single day.

My mind then begins flashing image after image: Breonna Taylor, the white nationalist rally in Charlottesville, the nine Black individuals who were killed in their church by a white supremacist whose name is not worth mentioning, Trayvon Martin, Tamir Rice, Philando Castile, Elijah McClain, and countless others. I think of Christian Cooper, who just wanted to go bird-watching in Central Park, but because his humanity was clothed in Blackness, he was perceived as an immediate threat to a white woman whose entitlement and superiority complex led her to call the police to tell them an "African American man" was "threatening her and her dog." I think about the Historically Black Colleges and Universities and Black faith institutions targeted with bomb threats earlier this year, reminding every single Black person how targeted we are just because we are getting louder about the injustices we face.

I think of the devastating white supremacist–led mass shooting of Black people in a Buffalo supermarket that happened right as I was writing chapter 5. I remember how my heart sank when the news broke about this racist terrorist attack and how Great Replacement Theory was the reason behind it. I could barely continue writing that day because I couldn't stop the tears from clouding my vision as the very real realization that it is getting even more unsafe to be Black in America vehemently hit my soul.

I think about the chilling images of the January 6th insurrection and the incredibly rude awakening it provided as to *just how many* are relentlessly fighting to preserve white supremacy. I think about leaders of our country who proudly support this fight and run entire election campaigns on the promise to "Save America," which is just code for "Keep America white."

I think about how, since we have been forcing society to look at its white supremacist and racist foundations, we've experienced so much whitelash driven by the fear of loss of power that now we can't even teach a fragment of the truth of our history in schools, causing an even greater equity divide and a rise of both in-school racism and *suicide* driven by in-school racism. I think about every single BIPOC and LGBTQIA+ child who will be gravely afflicted by the recent bans of inclusive books and anti-racist education in schools—children who won't ever have their lived experiences amplified and represented just because the truth about those lived experiences may make white kids who've never had to face such marginalization a tad bit uncomfortable. I think about the ten-year-old girl in Utah who couldn't take the racist bullying she was receiving any longer and chose to permanently remove herself from ever having to deal with it again. I think about every child who goes to school every day wondering if that day will be their last.

I think about the racism our first Black woman Supreme Court justice had to endure just to be confirmed for the seat she was more qualified for than anyone else who was already sitting on the Supreme Court. I think about the trauma induced for Black women everywhere as we watched it happen on national television and recounted our own stories of similar experiences at our places of work or in pursuit of higher education—just to be gaslit and made to endure even more racism for sharing our truth.

My mind continues to be flooded with image after image and headline after headline. The brutal images of Haitian migrants being whipped by white men on horseback at the border. Black residents in Ukraine being attacked and prevented from escaping during Russia's invasion of the country just because they were Black. More innocent, unarmed Black people murdered by police, and many of those police not receiving any penalty for their crimes. The rise of anti-Asian and anti-Semitic hate crimes. Adam Toledo. A truckful of white nationalists caught by law enforcement as they were on their way to terrorize a Pride event. The rise of Christian Nationalism. The removal of the right for people with uteruses to make decisions about their own bodies in the name of power and control. Guns effectively having more rights than women.

We are in the midst of one of the biggest white supremacist backlashes in history, and every single time we have been met with backlash before, white supremacy has always found a way to win. Even though white supremacy harms every single one of us, it is still a system that directly advantages exactly who it was built to advantage, so it's no surprise that since many advocates are now fighting to dismantle the system as a whole, the fight to preserve the system is stronger than ever. Nevertheless, that doesn't make the realities of this whitelash any easier to face.

It's not easy to face at all. It's chilling. It's traumatizing. It's infuriating.

And sometimes it feels irreparable and incorrigible, and I can't help but wonder, *Is any of this really worth it?*

When I first entered this fight, I didn't expect it to feel like this. I didn't expect it to be *this* terrifying and oftentimes feel *this* demoralizing. I naively thought that this time, with all the evidence, videos, and protests, things would be different. More people were recognizing the truth about white supremacy, more people were talking about the effects of white supremacy culture, and more people were willing to join the conversation than ever before. More books were being read and more content was being shared online. I am far from the only person teaching about white supremacy culture and advocating for dismantling white supremacy as a whole, and that's a good thing. There *is* momentum with this movement, and I have seen many people experience an awakening as they allow themselves to learn these truths and open themselves up to unlearning their societal conditioning.

However, even with growing momentum across all color, gender, and age lines, those of us in this fight—I mean, truly fighting to dismantle white supremacy—are a minority. No matter how harmful white supremacy is, it is still a god that the majority of society worships, entranced by its false promises of prosperity, righteousness, and worthiness. And when there is an attack on anyone's god, no matter how dangerous or toxic that god is, the response will be violent. The uptick in white supremacist extremist groups, hate crimes, and overt racism are all in direct correlation to the threat that those of us fighting for liberation pose to those who feel their white power, and the white power of society, slipping between their fingertips.

I don't take your commitment to this fight lightly. Your being here gives me hope and keeps me going with this work that often feels insurmountable. Thank you for being here. Thank you for joining the fight not just for your own liberation but for the liberation of all of society.

I wish I could tell you that you will see progress every day. I wish I could tell you that there will be more days of progress than there will be steps backward. I wish I could tell you that you'll encounter more open minds than closed ones and you'll never face hatred for joining this fight. I wish I could tell you that you'll never have to shed angry tears when it feels like no matter how hard you fight, society continues to regress. I wish I could tell you that this fight will end in our lifetimes and we'll be able to experience a society that has demolished white supremacy once and for all.

I wish I could tie that nice, lovely bow around this story, one which you and I both deserve.

I can't. But I can tell you this fight is worth it. It is worth it because *you* are worth it.

We are worth it.

Humanity is worth it.

Dismantling the System

Permanent change cannot be made within the system that has harmed us.

For far too long, we've been trying to accomplish change *within* the system. We still are. Even many who claim to be advocates for dismantling white supremacy are still attempting to do so in ways that are just making alterations to the system itself. And that makes sense when it's all you've known. It makes sense when you're just one person and the mere thought of dismantling an entire system our society was founded upon over four hundred years ago feels like the most daunting and unattainable task ever. We are talking about a complete structure that is deeply embedded into every single aspect of our lives. The literal framework from which our livelihoods run.

None of us can wake up tomorrow and take a bulldozer to the system and call it a done deal, as much as I'm sure we all wish we could. That would not only be too easy but would actually be ineffective. As much as we all want to shout on social media that we just need to burn the entire frustrating system to the ground, we all know that our reliance on these systems makes that physically impossible. The dismantling of white supremacy must be done in a way that allows for society to continue to run while we deconstruct the system piece by piece. Think back to our house analogy. I want you to imagine deconstructing the house of white supremacy as if starting from the very top of the roof and slowly working down to the foundation. Piece by piece, brick by brick, we must steadily and methodically begin taking down the house.

Now remember, this house is huge. *Huge.* Imagine one house covering the entire Western world. That's how huge we are talking. There is more than enough room for each of us to take a place on the roof and begin taking it apart. Right now, that looks like starting right where you are with your direct spheres of influence, which are whatever institutions or group settings you associate with regularly. These include your place of work, your school, your church, your social clubs and organizations (for yourself and your children), and your household.

Every single institution, whether big or small, has a structure based on white supremacy and perpetuates white supremacy culture. The only exempt institutions are those in parts of the world untouched by white supremacy. Your job is to discover what tenets of white supremacy exist within the institutions you frequent and begin the work of eradication.

The Tenets of White Supremacy to Look For

The tenets of white supremacy are much like its cultural characteristics. We'll work through which cultural characteristics are associated with which tenet so that you can begin to identify the primary tenets existing within your affiliated institutions based on what characteristics you see. Much of this material is interpreted from the great work of Dr. Tema Okun.[1]

1. **Patriarchy**

    Cultural characteristics: paternalism, power hoarding, hierarchy, perfectionism, objectivity, binary thinking, one right way.

    In a patriarchal institution, deference and preference are always given to male figures. Male figures are more often seen as leaders while female figures are treated as subordinates. Masculine energy is respected and appreciated while feminine energy is looked down upon as weak and docile. Typically, in patriarchal institutions, male figures are not only given more authority but also more freedom and preferential treatment, while female figures are controlled and seen as an inconvenience.

    The result of patriarchy is typically a demand for perfectionism and objectivity without any room for nuance, emotion, or humanity. Any behaviors that are considered "different" are considered wrong or something that needs correcting. Typically, behaviors that stem from feminine energy, such as emotions, sensitivity, and anxiety, fall in that "needs correction" category.

A patriarchal structure will ensure that (a) there is a power structure within the institution and (b) that power structure is unchangeable unless those seeking power are essentially clones of those already in power. Those who hold the power in a patriarchal institution will typically abuse that power—intentionally causing harm to those beneath them just because they can.

An example of how patriarchy shows up in the home is often between parents and children. Parents tend to believe that because they hold the power, children must submit to that power without question. Children's emotions are seen as inconvenient, their opinions may not be valued, and decisions are often made without their say-so. Children may be given less grace for error even when those in power make just as many, if not more, errors themselves.

2. **Ableism**

Cultural characteristics: perfectionism, one right way, qualifications, binary thinking.

An ableist institution is one that caters to those who are able-bodied, othering those with disabilities and treating them as inconveniences. Ableism declares that an abled body is "correct" and a disabled body is "incorrect." If you are able-bodied, then you are superior and have immediate justification to scoff at those who are disabled and not create an equitable environment for them.

Demanding perfectionism is ableist because standards of perfection are set by those who are able-bodied. This communicates that to be able-bodied and perform at the capacity an able-bodied person can is *the standard*. Requiring specific qualifications to perform generalized tasks or responsibilities is ableist, as those qualifications are typically more easily attainable in an abled body. Binary thinking is ableist as well as patriarchal because it doesn't allow for two things to be true at once. We are told we must always pick an answer, a feeling, or a response without being allowed to explore the nuances that always exist. For disabled bodies, "both/and" exists much more than "either/or," yet "both/and" is often shamed.

Ableism can occur even when no medically disabled people are present within the institution. For example, you can practice ableism within your home even if you don't have any disabled family members by simply not giving space when someone in your household feels sick, feels tired, needs a break, is struggling with mental health, and more. Ableism occurs any time any human condition outside of perfection is treated as an inconvenience or a weakness and is used against an individual.

3. **Capitalism**

   Cultural characteristics: prioritizing production, quantity over quality, individualism, worship of the written word, urgency.

   In a capitalistic institution, profit always comes before humanity. Profit doesn't necessarily mean monetary currency but also time, completion of a given task, or achievement of standards set by the institution. With capitalism, these currencies are seen as valuable, and humanity is seen as something worth sacrificing to obtain those currencies.

Capitalism breeds an obsession with progress and incites anxiety within ourselves whenever we feel as though progress is not being made. If we are perpetuating capitalism within our institutions, we are causing others anxiety and insecurity if we think they aren't making progress by whatever standards have been set.

That demand for constant progress leads to individualism—an individual feels shame for whatever lack of progress they've internalized and feels as though they must work extra hard without accepting help to complete tasks. Not to mention that the fierce competition capitalism demands from all of us breeds toxic individualism that causes us to treat our neighbors as enemies rather than teammates. Demand for progress also leads to a pursuit of more work being done (quantity) over making sure the work is done well (quality) to prove how valuable a person is. Quantity doesn't necessarily have to be numerical. This can also show up as taking shortcuts to get things done faster rather than taking time to do something with excellence or as finding a way to "cheat" to make progress look more impressive than it is.

Lastly, a capitalist institution values the worship of the written word, meaning that nothing is legitimate until it is written down on paper. This is a weird one, and typically only takes place in workplaces, but it is still important. Essentially, your word is not valued unless it is in a memo. Access to crucial resources is often not granted unless paperwork is involved. Research and evidence are typically valued more than opinion and human experience.

Capitalism rears its ugly head in our homes when we're more concerned with whether our kids finish their chores than we are with protecting their playtime. We often treat everything as transactional—children aren't allowed to have a treat or partake in something fun unless they have completed a checklist that proves they "deserved it." We give more deference and importance to education and homework than rest and enjoyment. We think that since there is only one right way to do things, we must be *the only ones* who can get those things done and that no one else is reliable.

4. **Heterosexism**

   Cultural characteristics: paternalism, binary thinking, right to comfort, one right way.

Heterosexism runs rampant in all of our institutions as we have been conditioned to believe that heterosexual affiliation is the norm and that anything else is othered and inferior. This belief teaches a justification of discrimination against members of the LGBTQIA+ community as well as support for legislation that further marginalizes this community. An example of this behavior in many religious institutions is found in the catchphrase "Hate the sin, love the sinner," which is just oppression disguised as acceptance.

In a heterosexist environment, paternalistic behaviors are once again considered superior and masculinity is only accepted when a male is the one exhibiting that behavior. In the home, we may see this play out when children exhibit behaviors and traits opposite of what their gender "norms" are, and those in power (the parents) fear these behaviors and try to put a stop to them instead of allowing children to express all sides of themselves fully. Heterosexism believes there are inherent gender norms (girls should do activities like dance, not sports like football; boys should play with action figures, not dolls) and refuses to believe these norms are completely constructed by society for gender and sexual oppression.

5. **Racism**

> *Cultural characteristics: all*, but especially defensiveness, right to comfort, fear of open conflict, power hoarding.

Racism is the founding tenet of white supremacy. Every single characteristic and tenet of white supremacy and white supremacy culture is rooted in racism. You know this. You read chapters 1–9, after all.

Your institution perpetuates racism anytime the characteristics and traits of whiteness or Eurocentric culture have been deemed the standard or the norm over all other cultural characteristics and traits. Your institution perpetuates racism when it is clear that power, preference, and hierarchy are given to individuals who are white versus BIPOC.

Your institution perpetuates racism when a mindset is carried that BIPOC societal challenges are due to a lack of personal merit rather than proven systemic racism; when white fragility, defensiveness, and fear of conflict become more important than the concerns of BIPOC; and when it refuses to dismantle white supremacy within it.

Racism and patriarchy go hand in hand because the abusive power of patriarchy helps enable the abusive power of white supremacy. Ableism is rooted in racism, as Blackness was originally (and is presently) viewed as nearly equivalent to disease and disability. Capitalism is rooted in racism as capitalism has always served as the currency of white supremacy and maintained power by exploiting the labor of the victims of racism. Heterosexism and racism intersect as they both stem from the belief that there is a universal norm or *standard* way of living and anything that falls outside of that standard is inferior and *deserves the oppression it receives.*

You begin dismantling white supremacy when you begin rejecting and dismantling these tenets, or systems of oppression, that exist under the umbrella of white supremacy within the institutions you associate with. It's easy to think that as individuals we have no power, as the overall power within our society sits with the wealthy, the elite, and those in legislative positions. However, we all have much more power than we give ourselves credit for. We have institutions within our reach that embolden white supremacy that we have the power to dismantle. Our dismantling will have a domino effect, leading others to dismantle the systems within their reach, and so on.

Eventually, these changes will reach people in positions of power. That power doesn't have to be the White House or Parliament or any other top political position. It shouldn't start there. When the dominoes reach our school boards, our city councils, and our church advisory boards, we are going to experience so much liberating change. It's going to be more transformational than we ever imagined.

We often want to believe change won't happen unless those at the very top force it to happen. And when that doesn't happen, we continue to sit in our frustration, stewing in anger as our hopelessness increases. Yes, we need the dismantling of white supremacy to reach the very top of the power hierarchy, but we have to stop focusing on the top as the only way to demolish this system. The majority of the demolition must take place within the institutions we interact with daily. This is where we will experience the most immediate impact. I don't mean this to say that the difference will be instantaneous, but it is the most immediate way we can make change that will have the most widespread effect. The political and economic framework that is the foundation of our societal structure will not change until we reject its influence on every other institution within our society, leaving no choice but for it to follow suit.

What Dismantling Will Look Like

We've discussed what it looks like when the various tenets of white supremacy show up within our institutions. Now let's talk about the antidotes to those tenets so we have physical examples of what it looks like to change the systems.

1. **Patriarchy Antidotes**

   The antidote to patriarchy is sharing power as well as equally valuing both masculine and feminine characteristics, energy, and traits. A culture of endless support is the only culture that exists. Toxic hierarchy is eliminated and work is collaborative. Within a healthy hierarchy, those in power only use their power to uplift, amplify, and empower those "beneath" them. They do not exploit others' labor or abuse their power, and the relationship between them and their constituents is one where all are valued equally.

   Note: sexism falls under patriarchy. Sexism has no place in an anti-patriarchal institution.

2. **Ableism Antidotes**

   The antidote to ableism is the eradication of perfectionism and every other closely associated characteristic. Abled bodies are not considered the norm and disabled bodies are not othered; instead, everybody has differing abilities and a culture is created where those abilities are celebrated, supported, and accommodated. Binary thinking and believing there is one right way of doing things are eliminated. Most importantly, humanity is prioritized, always. There is no expectation to perform or produce when one is not at their best. Space is made for rest, recovery, and play, as those are not seen as frivolous pursuits.

3. **Capitalism Antidotes**

In an anti-capitalist institution, labor is no longer exploited for the gain of the powerful, and humanity is never, ever placed after profit and productivity. Period. Wealth is shared more equitably among workers instead of hoarded by those at the top of the hierarchy (who often do little to execute the plans that increase production and revenue). The goal is creating a culture that values and prioritizes humanity instead of perfection and endless production.

4. **Heterosexism Antidotes**

Here, there are no gender or sexual orientation norms and no one is othered. Yes, even in faith institutions. *Especially* in faith institutions. The only norm is that God created each person in his image and likeness, making no mistakes and citing no rules that women must wear pink and men must wear blue. Gender expression is in the eye of the beholder, the only sexual norm is loving and non-abusive relationships, and superiority among genders and sexual orientations does not exist.

5. **Racism Antidotes**

In an anti-racist institution, anti-Blackness is destroyed. Blackness, and one's proximity to it, does not equal threatening, ugly, unintelligent, inferior, or any other in-furiating racist idea that has shaped our world. Whiteness is not the standard. I repeat: *whiteness is not the standard.* Equitable measures are put in place to correct the systemic injustices against the Black population that have been perpetuated since 1619. That means color-blindness isn't enough. Equality isn't enough. Holding hands and singing "Kumbaya" will not cut it. We must *reverse* the detriments of racism once and for all. We must hand over power, cre-ate opportunities, pay reparations, and break down sys-temic barriers that have kept BIPOC communities from flourishing.

You can do this. *We* can do this. I firmly believe we were born for such a time as this. I know I said that earlier, but it is true and bears repeating. Everything we have gone through thus far has led us to this very moment. We've been tasked with destroying the systems of oppression built in the name of Jesus that hurt Jesus's heart. Jesus didn't call us to make disciples of all nations by participating in and perpetuating systems of oppression and control and slapping his name on them, yet that has been the narrative of much of Chris-tianity since modernity (and most recently, Western civilization). We are called to *live justly, love mercy, and walk humbly with our God.*[2] That is it. It's honestly that simple. And Jesus showed us exactly how to do that when he walked this earth.

He eradicated systems of oppression. He called out the oppres-sors. He protested injustices. He obliterated power structures. He advocated for women and marginalized racial/ethnic communities. Now it is our turn. White supremacy is not the will of Jesus. It never has been, and it never will be.

Freedom

The fight has started with us.

We've confronted the lies that white supremacy brainwashed us with. We've found the root of those lies and are digging those roots out of our spirits once and for all. We're breaking free from white supremacy culture within ourselves, declaring the liberation that no one can take from us. We're healing from the wounds left by white supremacy and its trauma imposed on us and our ancestors, demanding that the generational trauma ends here.

Now we're taking our power back and dismantling white supremacy right where we are. We know that our power is more than enough and that, by being faithful, our power will be multiplied. We have the tools we need, and we are committed to our freedom.

And we'll all be free.

Journal Prompts

1. Within what institutions/spheres of influence can you commit to working to dismantle white supremacy?

2. Within those institutions, what tenets of white supremacy culture do you see most at play?

3. How have the tenets of white supremacy culture demonstrated themselves within your spheres of influence? What characteristics have you noticed?

4. How have you played a role in perpetuating white supremacy culture in your institutions? Where do you need to call yourself out?

5. How will you begin dismantling white supremacy culture within each of your spheres of influence? List the antidotes and *how* you will put them into practice.

Commitment to Freedom Statement

Write your commitment to freedom statement below. Include what you have learned about white supremacy and white supremacy culture, how white supremacy culture has impacted you, and your breakup with the culture. Also include your commitment to healing and breaking generational strongholds and dismantling the system as a whole. How will you go forward from the moment you close this book and live a life committed to your liberation and the liberation of all humankind?

_____

_____

_____

_____

_____

_____

_____

_____

_____

Epilogue

It's that bittersweet moment. The book has ended. You're moments away from closing it for good. Well, hopefully not for good. I hope you come back often. I'll be here when you need me. But on the other hand, I hope you don't come back too often. I hope you're diving into the life you're now free to live. I hope you're enjoying the liberated fruits of your labor.

I also hope you're reading more books. As much as I would have loved to be able to give you every single tool you'll ever need to divest yourself of white supremacy culture and dismantle it within society, I cannot. There is a plethora of other books, resources, speakers, workshops, and so much more that will give you additional tools for your toolbelt, depending on what you need. I've done some of the heavy lifting for you by compiling a list of my most recommended books in the following For Further Reading section. These include more resources about white supremacy, toxic patriarchy within the Christian church, understanding whiteness, deeper dives into the origins of racism, and more. Just like your healing is a lifetime of work, so will be your dismantling. And since this is a lifelong journey, you should consider yourself a lifelong student.

There is always more to learn and unlearn. There are always more discoveries to make. There are always more pieces to assemble. The more tools you possess, the more prepared you will be when life smacks you in the face and reminds you that you are still living in a dominant culture of white supremacy. You have to be armed and guarded. Remember, white supremacy does not like it when you try to fight against it. Your mirror will try to trick you back into falling for whiteness beauty standards. Your brain will try to slip back into perfectionism, urgency, and the need to constantly achieve rather than prioritizing rest and enjoyment without guilt. The news will remind you that white supremacy is still running rampant when the next headline takes your breath away, leaving you no choice but to sit there and sob before taking a few deep breaths and getting back at it.

It is okay to get knocked down. It is okay to need to take a break, or two, or twenty. In fact, breaks are encouraged. It's okay if you need to yell and scream and cry every other day just to get yourself through the toughest parts of this journey. Just make sure that you always get back in the ring. The moment you throw in the towel on the fight is the moment you throw in the towel on yourself. And you don't deserve that.

You may be wondering, *What's different this time, Caroline? We've seen what happens every time white supremacy is challenged—it always wins. How will this fight be any different?*

I'd be lying if I said I haven't asked myself this same question. White supremacy often feels entirely too big to conquer. Then God reminds me about David and Goliath. With David's faith in God, he had everything he needed to conquer Goliath right in his shepherd's bag. As significant in size and power as Goliath was, it took just one stone to the forehead to knock him down, giving David the advantage to then take Goliath's sword and finish the job.

We have the tools in our shepherd's bag—the tools to knock down white supremacy for good. And our faith will multiply the power of our tools, igniting a wildfire within our spheres of influence. Our job is to be faithful, to be committed, and to trust the process.

In every single fight for humanity in history, those who were on the front lines didn't get to see the results of the battles they won. Some didn't even find out they won the battle on this side of heaven. The majority of abolitionists didn't see the emancipation of slavery. Harriet Tubman never knew the impact she would make when she transported so many enslaved people to freedom.[1] The children and grandchildren of Dr. Martin Luther King Jr. are continuing the legacy he left but never got to witness for himself.[2] Those who have fought these fights just threw the stone they were tasked to throw. They focused on the battle they were called to fight. They didn't know how it would turn out, and more than likely, they didn't get to live to see the real fruits of their faith. Their faith and their commitment were their focus. The results were not their responsibility.

The results are also not our responsibility. And more than likely, we will not live to see the grand outcome of this fight. We are merely receiving the baton from those who came before us, adding our new tools and strategies to the battle (dismantling the actual system instead of trying to fix things *within* the system) and running forward as well as we can. And when our time is done, we will pass the baton onward, trusting that our efforts will not be in vain. We are planting seeds for our grandchildren's children, just as we have been able to reap the harvest of seeds planted just a few generations ago.

Let's not forget there is a major difference this time, though. The battle of generations prior relied on the legal changes they were fighting for before they could declare (some of) their freedom. This time, we're declaring our freedom first. No matter what rules society tries to enforce, we are free from that bondage. We get to reap that portion of the harvest immediately, and though it will be hard sometimes, no one can take that liberation from us.

And because we have finally discovered that the missing piece of the puzzle all along has been the need to demolish the system altogether rather than hope a few tweaks will cut it, this battle will forever be different from the ones that came before. I have faith that this will finally be the time white supremacy is knocked down for good. Just like Goliath.

Every single human being deserves the liberation you have just received.

Every single human being deserves to learn that they have always been worthy; it's our society that has brainwashed them into believing otherwise.

Every single human being deserves to be released from the bondage of white supremacy.

Every single human being deserves to be free.

―――

No matter how difficult, no matter how many times it feels impossible, the fight for freedom is always worth it.

The fight for freedom is *always* worth it.

For Further Reading

Candice Marie Benbow, *Red Lip Theology: For Church Girls Who've Considered Tithing to the Beauty Supply Store When Sunday Morning Isn't Enough*

Anthea Butler, *White Evangelical Racism: The Politics of Morality in America*

Christena Cleveland, *God Is a Black Woman*

Jasmine L. Holmes, *Carved in Ebony: Lessons from the Black Women Who Shape Us*

Jasmine L. Holmes, *Mother to Son: Letters to a Black Boy on Identity and Hope*

Angel Jones, *Street Scholar: Using Public Scholarship to Educate, Advocate, and Liberate*

Ibram X. Kendi, *How to Be an Antiracist*

Ibram X. Kendi, *Stamped from the Beginning: The Definitive History of Racist Ideas in America*

Ibram X. Kendi and Keisha N. Blain, eds., *Four Hundred Souls: A Community History of African America*

Chrissy King, *The Body Liberation Project: How Understanding Racism and Diet Culture Helps Cultivate Joy and Build Collective Freedom*

Duke L. Kwon and Gregory Thompson, *Reparations: A Christian Call for Repentance and Repair*

Heather McGhee, *The Sum of Us: What Racism Costs Everyone and How We Can Prosper Together*

Jenny Booth Potter, *Doing Nothing Is No Longer an Option: One Woman's Journey into Everyday Antiracism*

Layla F. Saad, *Me and White Supremacy: Combat Racism, Change the World, and Become a Good Ancestor*

Clint Smith, *How the Word Is Passed: A Reckoning with the History of Slavery Across America*

Danté Stewart, *Shoutin' in the Fire: An American Epistle*

Sabrina Strings, *Fearing the Black Body: The Racial Origins of Fat Phobia*

Tara Teng, *Your Body Is a Revolution: Healing Our Relationships with Our Bodies, Each Other, and the Earth*

Meghan Tschanz, *Women Rising: Learning to Listen, Reclaiming Our Voice*

Acknowledgments

A special thank-you to:

My agent, for seeing something in me that I didn't see in myself
and pushing me to see it too.

My editor, for believing in this work, believing in my capabilities to produce this work, and bringing out the best in my
writing.

My publishing team, for working tirelessly to bring this beautiful work to life.

My college best friends, for cheering me on every step of the
way.

My colleague, friend, and sister, for being a sounding board
and word of encouragement every time I wanted to quit.

My faithful online community, without whom I would not be
able to do this work.

Notes

Prelude

1. Vann R. Newkirk II, "The Language of White Supremacy," *Atlantic*, October 6, 2017, https://www.theatlantic.com/politics/archive/2017/10/the-language-of-white-supremacy/542148/.

2. Merriam-Webster Dictionary, s.v. "culture," accessed October 3, 2022, https://www.merriam-webster.com/dictionary/culture.

3. Tema Okun, "(Divorcing) White Supremacy Culture," Dismantling Racism Works, May 2021, https://www.dismantlingracism.org/white-supremacy-culture.html.

Chapter 1 Our Primal Wound

1. Nancy Newton Verrier, *The Primal Wound: Understanding the Adopted Child* (Baltimore, MD: Gateway Press, 2003).

2. Sarah Peterson, "How Early Childhood Trauma Is Unique," The National Child Traumatic Stress Network, March 23, 2018, https://www.nctsn.org/what-is-child-trauma/trauma-types/early-childhood-trauma/effects.

3. Dawn Davenport, "What Adoptive Parents Need to Know about the Primal Wound," Creating a Family, March 30, 2022, https://creatingafamily.org/adoption-category/adoptive-parents-primal-wound-2/.

4. "What Is Childhood Trauma?," Look through Their Eyes, accessed August 6, 2022, https://lookthroughtheireyes.org/what-is-childhood-trauma/.

5. Google Dictionary, Oxford Languages, s.v. "primal," accessed October 4, 2022, https://tinyurl.com/bdfrewpj.

6. Google Dictionary, Oxford Languages, s.v. "wound," accessed October 4, 2022, https://tinyurl.com/ydhchw6b.

7. Jered Brown, "Disproportionality and Race Equity in Child Welfare," National Conference of State Legislatures, accessed August 8, 2022, https://www.ncsl.org

/research/human-services/disproportionality-and-race-equity-in-child-welfare
.aspx.

8. LaKeisha Fleming, "The Foster Care System Disproportionately Affects Black
Children," Verywell Family, July 27, 2022, https://www.verywellfamily.com/foster
-care-system-inequities-affect-black-kids-5216184.

Chapter 3 Never Enough

1. Newkirk, "Language of White Supremacy," emphasis added.

2. Tema Okun, "(Divorcing) White Supremacy Culture: Coming Home to Who
We Really Are," White Supremacy Culture, accessed October 7, 2022, www.white
supremacyculture.info.

3. Tema Okun, "About Dismantling Racism Works," Drworksbook, accessed
October 7, 2022, https://www.dismantlingracism.org/about-drworks.html.

4. Tema Okun, "White Supremacy Culture Characteristics," White Supremacy
Culture, accessed October 7, 2022, www.whitesupremacyculture.info/characteris
tics.html.

5. Robert P. Baird, "The Invention of Whiteness: The Long History of a Dangerous Idea," *Guardian*, April 21, 2021, https://www.theguardian.com/news/2021/apr
/20/the-invention-of-whiteness-long-history-dangerous-idea.

6. Ibram X. Kendi, *Stamped from the Beginning: The Definitive History of Racist
Ideas in America* (New York: Bold Type Books, 2016), 17.

7. Kendi, *Stamped from the Beginning*, 17.

8. Kendi, *Stamped from the Beginning*, 17.

9. Kendi, *Stamped from the Beginning*, 23.

10. Kendi, *Stamped from the Beginning*, 22.

11. Kendi, *Stamped from the Beginning*, 22.

12. Kendi, *Stamped from the Beginning*, 23.

13. Kendi, *Stamped from the Beginning*, 23.

14. Kendi, *Stamped from the Beginning*, 23–25.

15. Kendi, *Stamped from the Beginning*, 24–25.

16. Ta-Nehisi Coates, *Between the World and Me* (New York: Spiegel & Grau,
2015), 7.

17. Kendi, *Stamped from the Beginning*, 16.

18. Kendi, *Stamped from the Beginning*, 6, 33.

19. Kendi, *Stamped from the Beginning*, 68–69, 75.

20. Kendi, *Stamped from the Beginning*, 41.

21. Louis Menand, "Morton, Agassiz, and the Origins of Scientific Racism in
the United States," *The Journal of Blacks in Higher Education* 34 (Winter 2001–02):
110–13; Kendi, *Stamped from the Beginning*, 179.

22. Menand, "Morton, Agassiz, and the Origins of Scientific Racism," 110.

23. Cara Nguyen, "The Relationship Between White Supremacy and Capitalism," *Seattle University Undergraduate Research Journal* (2020): 8.

24. "U.S. History Primary Source Timeline: Rise of Industrial America, 1876–
1900," Library of Congress, accessed October 7, 2022, https://www.loc.gov/class

room-materials/united-states-history-primary-source-timeline/rise-of-industrial
-america-1876-1900/.

25. Eric Niiler, "How the Second Industrial Revolution Changed Americans' Lives," *History*, January 25, 2019, https://www.history.com/news/second-industrial -revolution-advances.

26. Cara Letofsky, "Racism Killed the New Deal (and Gave Us Neoliberalism)," *An Injustice Magazine*, September 15, 2021, https://aninjusticemag.com/racism -killed-the-new-deal-and-gave-us-neoliberalism-1c794a8f2154.

27. Richard Rothstein, *The Color of Law: A Forgotten History of How Our Government Segregated America* (New York: Liveright, 2017).

28. Willow Lung-Amam, "The Next New Deal Must Be for Black Americans, Too," *Bloomberg*, January 18, 2021, https://www.bloomberg.com/news/articles/2021 -01-18/the-next-new-deal-must-be-for-black-americans-too.

29. Lung-Amam, "The Next New Deal Must Be for Black Americans, Too."

30. Lung-Amam, "The Next New Deal Must Be for Black Americans, Too."

31. Tim Boyd, "The 1966 Election in Georgia and the Ambiguity of White Backlash," *The Journal of Southern History* 75, no. 2 (May 2009): 305–40.

32. Raymond Pierce, "The Racist History of School Choice," *Forbes*, May 6, 2021, https://www.forbes.com/sites/raymondpierce/2021/05/06/the-racist-history-of -school-choice/?sh=2771e7fd6795; Kendi, *Stamped from the Beginning*, 240–45.

33. Heather McGhee, *The Sum of Us: What Racism Costs Everyone and How We Can Prosper Together* (Random House Audio, 2020); Letofsky, "Racism Killed the New Deal."

34. Letofsky, "Racism Killed the New Deal."

35. Letofsky, "Racism Killed the New Deal."

36. Letofsky, "Racism Killed the New Deal."

37. Joshua Zeitz, "What Everyone Gets Wrong about LBJ's Great Society," *Politico*, January 28, 2018, https://www.politico.com/magazine/story/2018/01/28/lbj -great-society-josh-zeitz-book-216538.

38. Zeitz, "What Everyone Gets Wrong."

39. Kendi, *Stamped from the Beginning*, 410–23; Equal Justice Initiative, "Nixon Advisor Admits War on Drugs Was Designed to Criminalize Black People," EJI, March 25, 2016, https://eji.org/news/nixon-war-on-drugs-designed-to-criminalize -black-people/.

40. Letofsky, "Racism Killed the New Deal."

41. Letofsky, "Racism Killed the New Deal."

42. Letofsky, "Racism Killed the New Deal."

43. Letofsky, "Racism Killed the New Deal"; Kendi, *Stamped from the Beginning*, 410–23.

44. Letofsky, "Racism Killed the New Deal."

45. Letofsky, "Racism Killed the New Deal."

46. Deborah M. Keisch, "U.S. Education Reform and the Maintenance of White Supremacy through Structural Violence," *Landscapes of Violence* 3, no. 3 (May 2015): 5–7.

47. Letofsky, "Racism Killed the New Deal."

Chapter 4 Where We First Learned to Be White

1. Ward Churchill, *Kill the Indian, Save the Man: The Genocidal Impact of American Indian Residential Schools* (San Francisco: City Lights Publishers, 2004).

2. Jessica Fu and Jimin Khan, "30 Million Children Rely on Free School Lunch. Where Do They Eat When School's Out?," *The Counter*, July 3, 2018, https://the counter.org/summer-hunger-new-york-city/.

3. Matthew Desmond, "In Order to Understand the Brutality of American Capitalism, You Have to Start on the Plantation," *New York Times Magazine*, August 14, 2019, https://www.nytimes.com/interactive/2019/08/14/magazine/slavery -capitalism.html.

4. Pierce, "The Racist History of School Choice"; Kendi, *Stamped from the Beginning*, 240.

5. Kendi, *Stamped from the Beginning*, 361–64.

6. Pierce, "Racist History of School Choice"; Kendi, *Stamped from the Beginning*, 240.

7. Pierce, "Racist History of School Choice"; Kendi, *Stamped from the Beginning*, 240.

8. Keisch, "U.S. Education Reform."

9. John Rosales and Tim Walker, "The Racist Beginnings of Standardized Testing," *NEA Today*, March 20, 2021, https://www.nea.org/advocating-for-change/new -from-nea/racist-beginnings-standardized-testing.

10. Rosales and Walker, "Racist Beginnings of Standardized Testing."

11. Rosales and Walker, "Racist Beginnings of Standardized Testing."

12. Dani Bostick, "The Classical Roots of White Supremacy," *Learning for Justice Magazine* 66 (Spring 2021); Lateisha Ugwuegbula, "The Role of Education in Perpetuating Racism and White Supremacy: Rethinking the Eurocentric Curriculum," Samuel Centre for Social Connectedness, July 2, 2020, https://www.socialconnected ness.org/the-role-of-education-in-perpetuating-racism-and-white-supremacy-re thinking-the-eurocentric-curriculum/.

Chapter 5 U.G.L.Y.

1. Mikeisha Vaughn, "Ghetto Until Proven Fashionable," *Essence*, November 4, 2020, https://www.essence.com/fashion/black-culture-ghetto-until-proven -fashionable/; Cady Lang, "*Keeping Up with the Kardashians* Is Ending. But Their Exploitation of Black Women's Aesthetics Continues," *TIME*, June 10, 2021, https:// time.com/6072750/kardashians-blackfishing-appropriation/.

2. Sabrina Strings, *Fearing the Black Body: The Racial Origins of Fat Phobia* (New York: New York University Press, 2019), 13.

3. Dr. Bryan Zygmont, "Venus of Willendorf," Khan Academy, accessed October 7, 2022, https://www.khanacademy.org/humanities/prehistoric-art/paleolithic /paleolithic-objects/a/venus-of-willendorf.

4. Zygmont, "Venus of Willendorf."

5. Bruno Maddox, "The Math Behind Beauty," *Discover Magazine*, June 1, 2007, https://www.discovermagazine.com/the-sciences/the-math-behind-beauty.

6. Strings, *Fearing the Black Body*, 29, 34–35, 46.

7. Strings, *Fearing the Black Body*, 12.

8. Strings, *Fearing the Black Body*, 69–98.

9. Strings, *Fearing the Black Body*, 44–45, 78.

10. Strings, *Fearing the Black Body*, 12; Brian Gallagher, "Racist Ideology and Black Abnormality in the Birth of a Nation," *Phylon (1960–)* 43, no. 1 (1982): 68–76.

11. Strings, *Fearing the Black Body*, 99–120.

12. Strings, *Fearing the Black Body*, 62, 79.

13. Strings, *Fearing the Black Body*, 20.

14. Strings, *Fearing the Black Body*, 59.

15. Strings, *Fearing the Black Body*, 69–98.

16. Strings, *Fearing the Black Body*, 69–98.

17. Strings, *Fearing the Black Body*, 82.

18. Strings, *Fearing the Black Body*, 98.

19. Strings, *Fearing the Black Body*, 99–120.

20. Strings, *Fearing the Black Body*, 121.

21. Adele Jackson-Gibson, "The Racist and Problematic History of the Body Mass Index," *Good Housekeeping*, February 23, 2021, https://www.goodhousekeep ing.com/health/diet-nutrition/a35047103/bmi-racist-history/.

22. Jackson-Gibson, "Racist and Problematic History."

23. Sarah Schwartz, "White Characters Still Dominate Kids' Books and School Texts, Report Finds," *EducationWeek*, December 1, 2021, https://www.edweek.org /teaching-learning/white-characters-still-dominate-kids-books-and-school-texts -report-finds/2021/12.

24. Jackson-Gibson, "Racist and Problematic History."

25. Jackson-Gibson, "Racist and Problematic History."

26. Jackson-Gibson, "Racist and Problematic History."

Chapter 6 Hustle

1. Peter Marks, "Shakespeare Wrote King Lear During a Plague. What Great Work Will Emerge from This Pandemic?" *Washington Post*, November 6, 2020, https://www.washingtonpost.com/entertainment/theater_dance/great-artistic -works-during-plagues/2020/11/05/6575cac2-1d29-11eb-90dd-abd0f7086a91 _story.html.

2. "COVID-19: Essential Workers in the States," National Conference of State Legislatures, January 11, 2021, https://www.ncsl.org/research/labor-and-employ ment/covid-19-essential-workers-in-the-states.aspx.

3. Erin Carson and Ian Sherr, "'Hustle Culture' Is Facing an Existential Crisis with Millennials," CNET, January 4, 2022, https://www.cnet.com/culture/hustle -culture-is-facing-an-existential-crisis-with-millennials/.

4. Cara Nguyen, "The Relationship Between White Supremacy and Capitalism: A Socioeconomic Study on Embeddedness in the Market and Society," *Seattle University Undergraduate Research Journal* 4 (2020), https://scholarworks.seattleu .edu/suurj/vol4/iss1/6/.

5. Desmond, "In Order to Understand the Brutality."

6. Desmond, "In Order to Understand the Brutality"; P. R. Lockhart, "How Slavery Became America's First Big Business," Vox, August 16, 2019, https://www.vox.com/identities/2019/8/16/20806069/slavery-economy-capitalism-violence-cotton-edward-baptist.

7. Desmond, "In Order to Understand the Brutality"; Lockart, "How Slavery Became America's First Big Business."

8. *Gilmore Girls*, season 2, episode 2, "Hammers and Veils," directed by Michael Katleman, written by Amy Sherman-Palladino, aired October 9, 2001, on The WB.

9. Ephesians 2:10; 4:11.

10. Malinda Fuller, "Hustle, Rest and the Real Example of Jesus," *Relevant*, March 1, 2021, https://relevantmagazine.com/life5/hustle-rest-and-real-example-jesus/.

11. Stephen Mattson, "Jesus Was a Protester," *Sojourners*, March 16, 2016, https://sojo.net/articles/jesus-was-protester.

12. Mattson, "Jesus Was a Protester"; Luke 4:16–31.

Chapter 7 The Crisis We Refuse to See

1. Matt Richtel, "'It's Life or Death': The Mental Health Crisis Among U.S. Teens," *New York Times*, April 23, 2022, https://www.nytimes.com/2022/04/23/health/mental-health-crisis-teens.html.

2. Dana Givens, "The Extra Stigma of Mental Health Illness for African Americans," *New York Times*, August 25, 2020, https://www.nytimes.com/2020/08/25/well/mind/black-mental-health.html; Richtel, "'It's Life or Death.'"

3. "Mental Health by the Numbers," National Alliance on Mental Illness, accessed October 7, 2022, https://www.nami.org/mhstats.

4. Kristen Rogers, "People of Color Face Significant Barriers to Mental Health Services," CNN, October 10, 2020, https://www.cnn.com/interactive/2020/10/health/mental-health-people-of-color-wellness/.

5. Rogers, "People of Color Face Significant Barriers."

6. Mental Health America, "The State of Mental Health in America," MHA, accessed October 7, 2022, https://mhanational.org/issues/state-mental-health-america.

7. Mental Health America, "State of Mental Health in America."

8. Tara Parker-Pope, Christina Caron, and Mónica Cordero Sancho, "Why 1,320 Therapists Are Worried about Mental Health in America Right Now," *New York Times*, December 16, 2021, https://www.nytimes.com/interactive/2021/12/16/well/mental-health-crisis-america-covid.html.

9. Mitchell J. Prinstein, "US Youth Are in a Mental Health Crisis—We Must Invest in Their Care," American Psychological Association, February 7, 2022, https://www.apa.org/news/press/op-eds/youth-mental-health-crisis.

10. *13th*, directed by Ava DuVernay, screenplay by Ava DuVernay and Spencer Averick (Kandoo Films, 2016).

11. See, for example, "Stop the Sexualization of Children Act of 2022," H. Res., 117th Cong. (2022), https://mikejohnson.house.gov/uploadedfiles/johnla_083_xml.pdf; Laurel Wamsley, "What's in the So-Called Don't Say Gay Bill That Could

Impact the Whole Country," NPR, October 21, 2022, https://www.npr.org/2022/10/21/1130297123/national-dont-say-gay-stop-children-sexualization-bill; Priya Krishnakumar and Devan Cole, "2022 Is Already a Record Year for State Bills Seeking to Curtail LGBTQ Rights, ALCU Data Shows," CNN, July 17, 2022, https://www.cnn.com/2022/07/17/politics/state-legislation-lgbtq-rights/index.html; Brandon Tensley, "'We're Seeing a Relaunch of an Old Story': Exploring the Movement to Ban Books with LGBTQ Characters," CNN, September 22, 2022, https://www.cnn.com/2022/09/22/us/lgbtq-book-bans-race-deconstructed-newsletter-reaj/index.html.

12. Ishena Robinson, "Anti-CRT Mania and Book Bans Are the Latest Tactics to Halt Racial Justice," Legal Defense Fund, accessed October 7, 2022, https://www.naacpldf.org/critical-race-theory-banned-books/.

13. Laura Hautala, "Amazon Adjusts 'Time Off Task' Policy That Critics Said Limited Bathroom Breaks," CNET, June 2, 2021, https://www.cnet.com/tech/tech-industry/amazon-adjusts-time-off-task-policy-that-critics-said-limited-bathroom-breaks/.

14. Jay Mathews, "Why Our Many Big Plans to Raise Education Standards Will Never Work," *Washington Post*, April 17, 2021, https://www.washingtonpost.com/local/education/common-core-education-standards/2021/04/16/dbedf91c-9c73-11eb-9d05-ae06f4529ece_story.html.

15. Luke 4:16–19.

Chapter 9 Breaking the Cycle

1. Fabiana Franco, "Understanding Intergenerational Trauma: An Introduction for Clinicians," *Good Therapy* (blog), January 8, 2021, https://www.goodtherapy.org/blog/Understanding_Intergenerational_Trauma.

Chapter 10 We'll All Be Free

1. Tema Okun, "White Supremacy Culture—Still Here," May 2021, https://drive.google.com/file/d/1XR_7M_9qa64zZ00_JyFVTAjmjVU-uSz8/view.

2. Micah 6:8.

Epilogue

1. "About Harriet Tubman," Harriet Tubman Byway, accessed October 7, 2022, https://harriettubmanbyway.org/harriet-tubman/.

2. Dr. Bernice A. King, "The King Center," The King Center, accessed November 7, 2022, https://thekingcenter.org.

Caroline J. Sumlin is a writer, speaker, and educator with a passion for helping all people to reclaim their self-worth and their humanity. A former foster child turned adoptee, Caroline brings awareness, healing, and liberation to the topics of toxic white supremacy culture, systemic injustice, mental health, faith reconstruction, and bold, purposeful living to her growing audience. She received her BA from Howard University and resides with her husband and two young daughters in northern Virginia.

Connect with
CAROLINE

CAROLINE J. SUMLIN
WRITER | SPEAKER | RULE BREAKER

CAROLINEJSUMLIN.COM

@carolinejsumlin